SURVIVAL MATH *for* MARKETERS

SURVIVAL MATH *for* MARKETERS

PETER C. WEIGLIN

University of California, Berkley

SAGE Publications
International Educational and Professional Publisher
Thousand Oaks ■ London ■ New Delhi

For information:

Sage Publications, Inc.
2455 Teller Road
Thousand Oaks, California 91320
E-mail: order@sagepub.com

Sage Publications Ltd.
6 Bonhill Street
London EC2A 4PU
United Kingdom

Sage Publications India Pvt. Ltd.
M-32 Market
Greater Kailash I
New Delhi 110 048 India

Printed in the United States of America

Library of Congress Cataloging-in-Publication Data

Weiglin, Peter C.
    Survival math for marketers / by Peter C. Weiglin.
        p. cm.
Includes bibliographical references.
    ISBN 0–7619–1632–6 (alk. paper)
    1. Marketing—Mathematics.   I. Title.
    HF5415 .W364 2002
    658'.001'51—dc21   2002005204

This book is printed on acid-free paper.

02 03 04 05 10 9 8 7 6 5 4 3 2 1

Acquisitions Editor: Marquita Flemming
Editorial Assistant: MaryAnn Vail
Copy Editor: Barbara Coster
Production Editor: Diane S. Foster
Typesetter: Graphicraft Limited, Hong Kong
Proofreader: Jamie Robinson
Cover Designer: Michelle Lee

Contents

Preface

This volume came about because a large number of the students in my Essentials of Marketing classes over the years demonstrated an abysmal knowledge of its contents. They were (and are) intelligent, competent, functioning professionals and executives in one or another of the marketing subdisciplines or in a technical area. But their prior training had not included a realistic grounding in accounting, finance, mathematics, or economics. The prototype examples are (a) English or psychology majors who are now responsible for all or part of the promotion/advertising effort at a company and (b) engineers who have become involved in the sales/business side of their organization.

To put it mildly, these folks suddenly found themselves floundering in an unfamiliar world, not fully understanding the bases on which they were being judged, and too often being blindsided by mathematical forces that, they were assured, were beyond their control.

Hence this book, which will not teach you everything about the mathematical disciplines related to marketing and management, but will get you started, fill in some gaps, or explain a few things that may have been puzzling you.

Part of what we're doing is identifying problems that aren't math problems at all, but people problems. Like price sensitivity or product distribution or sales estimates.

There are math tools that can help you, but they are neither magic answers nor ends in themselves. In fact, for just about every "math problem," when you scratch it, you'll find a people problem hidden underneath.

This book explores that relationship between math and people. What are "generally accepted accounting principles"? Why is this or that formula or apportionment method being used? How much did that widget really cost us? How does all of this square with our personal code of ethics?

Many people have contributed to this effort, and I know I'll never have room to name them all. The list includes Rajiv Samantrai, Callee Brown, Judy Rothman, Sarah Hawthorne, and Jeanne Weiglin. The list also includes a number of my past colleagues and adversaries whose actions formed the basis for statements that might otherwise have been thought to be unbelievable.

Finally, I must thank, and dedicate this volume to, three women who have contributed to the feminization of the accounting profession—

Dawn Weiglin Glover
Joanne Larson Short
Vera Harries Wall

—all of whom substantiate my statement that "Some of my relatives and best friends are accountants." They succeeded and are succeeding, because they understand the principles outlined in this book.

Peter C. Weiglin
San Mateo, California

One

Your Credibility

It's Absolute and Definite (Maybe)

Too many people hate finance and accounting numbers. What's worse, not enough marketing people understand financial and accounting concepts, and therefore, not enough marketing people are able to use these concepts and tools to improve the marketing focus of their organizations.

Upon being faced with financial statements, printouts, budgets, reports, and similar documents covered with numbers, many marketing people (and people from other "nonfinancial" disciplines) throw up their hands. With bad memories of math and accounting classes from school, they avoid contact with these things as much as possible. It's even called "math phobia" by some, which gives it an air of psychological legitimacy. The result is that far too many people opt out and render themselves incapable of deciphering even the most elementary financial statements. Then they wonder why something that looked so good could turn out to be so bad.

Now, these are, by and large, intelligent people. My sample even includes many graduate engineers, who are quite familiar with complex mathematical calculation, including integral calculus. But put dollar signs on the figures instead of exponents, and they go blank, or they withdraw. Common symptoms include statements such as, "That's a foreign language to me," or "That's for the bean counters to understand," or "I think we've got enough fat in our budget that they leave us alone." I have even heard, "We have a constant battle with the damned narrow-minded accountants, who don't understand the business."

1

Well, whether the number crunchers understand the business or not, they most certainly do understand the organization or company. Even though as marketing people we try our best to focus on the customer, it's inescapable that we must function as part of an organization. Unless you're the CEO (chief executive officer), you must gain approval of the CEO (or a person or committee he or she designates) for the expenditure of the organization's resources. This is most often done in the form of an approved plan and budget, against which performance is compared and monitored.

If you're the CEO, you soon find that you must gain approval from others, or at the very least develop support from others, for the projects you wish to undertake. And even the most individualistic CEOs learn that they disregard the advice of their financial people at their own peril.

Even people who have taken one or more accounting and finance classes, and who do understand many of the mechanics of accounting, have remained unaware of the degree to which the principles and methods used are subject to change and interpretation. The common understanding is that accounting is an exact science, that 2 plus 2 equals 4, that there is an objective reality to the financial process.

It ain't so. There is no single objective reality. The accounting profession swears that they are working toward a set of standards rooted in objective reality, but it isn't there, and it never will be. The basis for acceptable methods of recording and evaluation, and other "standards," is summed up in the phrase that auditors attach to annual reports: that the data are based on "generally accepted accounting principles." The American Institute of Certified Public Accountants and other groups have developed these standards over the years to meet the requirements of federal and state tax and securities laws and to satisfy a desire for comparability of financial statements from company to company.

The entire system of accounting has evolved over the years through a process of negotiation and compromise between various parties interested in knowing the results of business activity. That includes governments (particularly tax collectors) and investors. Unlike the physical sciences (or even the medical sciences), we are not discovering and analyzing pre-existing natural relationships and conditions. Rather, accounting is a tool that people have devised to keep track of human activity and to make it understandable to those who provide the capital that funds that activity.

The process has, over the years, developed some universally accepted ways of doing things. But in most cases, there is more than one "acceptable" approach or method for tackling a given accounting task. Are you on a cash or an accrual basis? Is your inventory valued using LIFO (Last In, First Out) or FIFO (First In, First Out), or something else? During what time period is a new sale credited: order date, sales acceptance date, initial ship date, or receipt date? How was the estimated annual cost of employee vacations determined? How are engineering costs allocated among the company's various products? By unit sales? By dollar sales? By direct costs? By total cost allocation?

A Few Definitions

To help prepare you to understand the financial side of the business, let us now consider a few "standard" definitions:

Business: an organization that provides a product or service

Marketing: the process whereby supplier production and customer demand come together in an exchange of value

Cost: money we expend to produce our product and operate our businesses

Revenue: money received in exchange for our product

Profit: excess of revenue over costs

Loss: negative profit, that is, insufficiency of revenue to cover costs

Accounting: the scientific method of recording, summarizing, and analyzing the financial impact of the business operations

Now, let's look at those same definitions in a "radical" way:

Business: an organization that generates and collects valid invoices that customers pay because their needs have been satisfied

Marketing: management of those resources that affect customer satisfaction

Cost: those resources we expend to identify, attract, and satisfy our customers

Revenue: money we receive from customers because we have satisfied their needs

Profit: the amount by which our customers believe our products to be worth more than the resources we expended on those products

Loss: the amount by which present and potential customers believe our products to be worth less than the resources we expended on those products

Accounting: the collectively agreed-upon process whereby the financial results of the company's operations are presented in the best possible light

Quite a difference in approach, isn't it? Note that what we believe, what we take for granted, is of no importance whatsoever. All that matters is what our customers believe. (Or what our shareholders believe.) This is at sharp variance with general tendencies in many businesses and organizations.

Why Is This Important to Me?

By now, you see that there are alternate approaches to many of the conditions that play a role in the rules and standards a company may follow. In personal terms, those accounting practices make up the standard by which you and your performance will be judged. All other measurements (sometimes called "metrics") and standards of your performance are subordinate to this one: Did you achieve a sufficient return on the resources invested in your activity?

The answer to that question involves many assumptions and decisions, which are often presented as unchangeable rules. Quite often, you are being judged on the basis of measurements that reflect your organization's situation a number of years ago. As I have noted, the point to remember is this: Every rule, every standard, every "correct" method of accounting was developed through a process of proposal and negotiation, followed by the CEO's and/or board of directors' approval. It may not even be the incumbent CEO who approved the "standard procedure"; it may date back to 1970, or earlier. Many of these procedures are followed because "that's the way we've always done it." Company custom and a decision made long ago become mistaken for unchangeable rule.

To succeed, we must take nothing for granted. I have seen cases in which costs have been allocated under formulas unchanged since World War II. My favorite was allocation of half of the central headquarters staff costs to a division that had been responsible for half of the company's sales when the allocation was made in 1985 but which now produced less than 10% of total revenue. (Why had it not been changed? You may rest assured that the managers of the other divisions thought the allocation as it stood was fair and equitable, and traditional, and they argued against making any change in the procedure. If you don't yet know why, read on.)

A Short True-False Quiz

Let's look at some of the underlying attitudes that govern business operations. Consider the following statements and decide whether each one is true or false.

1. The first consideration in any business is the resources of the firm.

2. The marketing function in our firm exists to provide support for the sales effort.

3. A long-range marketing budget isn't necessary because these efforts must be flexible to respond to competitive challenges in the marketplace.

4. Marketing people don't have to waste a lot of time understanding accounting; they just have to come up with great ideas based on what they're told.

5. The company's fiscal year is set by law and cannot be changed.

6. It is more important to keep up with our competitors' actions than it is to waste a lot of money on customer research that may not lead anywhere.

7. The price is by far our customers' most important consideration in making a buying decision.

8. The goal of any company should be to make its product so good that it sells itself. A superior product is more important than anything else we can do.

9. If there is a statistical correlation between two things, that indicates a definite relationship: cause and effect.

10. We understand our customers. The proof of that is that we have been in business for ___ years (fill in the blank).

11. Fancy packaging of a product just adds costs without helping the product.

12. The best predictor of the future is the trend in the recent past.

13. We control our costs better by not getting the advertising people involved until everything is done but the creative work.

Now for the answers:

They are all false. Every last one of them is false, as we will subsequently see. The problem is that in many organizations, people who you might think would know better are checking "True." Not you, of course; but perhaps your boss—or your boss's boss. Or perhaps the cretin in Administration or Accounting who keeps asking you dumb questions or telling you why things can't be done or why something is too costly.

Reality and Perception

Every successful marketing person knows that the key to customer satisfaction lies in understanding the perceptions of the customer. Different customers perceive the same product or marketing mix in different ways, which will most likely not agree with what we "know" to be true. Some people go so far as to say that if you stop and think about it, there is no such thing as objective reality.

Let me repeat that: It is wise to remember that where people are concerned, there is no such thing as objective reality. There is only a group of subjective evaluations by people who make decisions, based on their imperfect understanding of "reality," and each of those people is different. What looks to you and me like reality is nothing more than the collective, agreed-upon perception of a number of people, particularly the people in charge. Reality, then, may be described as "that subjective perception that has been commonly agreed upon or approved by higher authority."

For example, we take it for granted that we know our product best. And it's not too great a leap from there to convince ourselves that we know what's best for our customers, too. A well-known orchestra conductor was heard to say about his audience, "So, they do not like the music of Richard Wagner? Then we will play Wagner until they *love* Wagner." He was serious, and he had the orchestra play more Wagner, trying vainly to convince concertgoers that "Wagner's music wasn't as bad as it sounds," as one critic put it. The orchestra became the best performer of Wagnerian music in the country. But the resultant drop in ticket sales and donations from customers who rapidly tired of hearing Wagner almost bankrupted the orchestra until the conductor was replaced.

Regardless of what you may think is right, true, just, or brimming with common sense, the fact is that the *customer's* perception controls, and not what *we* "know" internally to be true or what we take for granted. The first consideration in any business is the customer, not the firm's capabilities or resources.

Even something as basic as the concept of "value" is not as simple as it appears at first. That's because different people attach different levels of value to a given product, depending on their circumstances. Note, by the way, that I did not say "value of *the same* product." Even the concept of whether a product is the same or not is going to vary between any two people.

Why should it be any different within an organization, given that the organization contains people, all with different perceptions? After all, every one of those managers who understands the concepts in this book will have been making the case for an accounting system that puts him or her in the best light. I believe that much of the confusion and aversion that surrounds financial reporting and analysis comes about because we have been told that the numbers are bedrock fact, whereas in fact they don't look like bedrock fact. Well, they aren't always bedrock fact. Knowing that, we can move forward and use the tools and the perceptions to work for us instead of against us.

The Numbers Control Us

It is presumed that the projects you are undertaking or wish to undertake will produce a profit for the company or, at the very least, will yield a result that is valuable enough to justify the expenditure of those resources committed to your activity. Success or failure will be judged on the basis of financial results. People may prattle on about the intangible benefits of a proposed expense: goodwill, happy customers, a better public image, positioning, better employee relations, and so on. But if those efforts don't translate into a better financial picture, "the numbers" will dictate that we not spend (waste) the money.

Furthermore, the person who keeps proposing projects and expenditures that are "good ideas," but who cannot demonstrate the vital link between a good idea and the organization's financial improvement, will soon be branded as an airhead by others in management, who will be reinforced by the accountants in that opinion. For the proposer of such projects, that means an accompanying lessening of effectiveness and a reduced chance of meaningful career advancement.

The tragedy is that the idea might have been quite profitable to the firm, yet the manner of its presentation may not have convinced the decision makers of its value. Somebody else's project got funded instead, because that other proposer made the sale by translating that other project into tangible dollar benefits for the firm.

Another problem is that your *boss* might not be aware of some of the material in this book, which can also have a negative effect on your career. I remember one manager who came from an academic environment (English literature). He had to be educated annually about budgets by a couple of his people. Every year, until his merciful departure, the poor man would ask, "Now, which of these numbers are the revenues?" After all, if your department or division continually loses those negotiation battles for available resources, your department is less likely to (a) perform well or (b) be regarded as a spawning ground for higher-level people.

It follows, therefore, that if you have an understanding of the numbers, how they get that way, and how people use them, then you will have a competitive advantage over those who do not understand. Let me put that another way: If you do not understand these numbers-related concepts, you will be had for lunch by those who do.

The truth is that nobody ever played a truly strategic role in the upper echelons of a company without understanding the concepts in this book. In any organization, the numbers are the means by which success or failure is measured. Note that the measurement itself is not objective, but subjective.

Will the Auditors Protect Us?

Not necessarily. Customers, suppliers, investors, and employees place great reliance on the idea that financial statements reviewed by independent auditors provide the truth, or at least enough truthful information upon which to make decisions about the company.

But revelations about companies such as Enron and Global Crossing have called the auditing process into question.

In the ideal sense, independent or outside auditors are retained by a company to inspect and review its financial policies, procedures, and transactions to ensure that the company and those who do business with it have an accurate picture of the company's finances. In every annual report, you will find the "Auditor's Letter," in which the outside auditor assures the world that the statements reflect "generally accepted accounting principles."

Two problems surface in this situation.

First, the idea of generally accepted accounting principles allows for some variance in exactly what is "generally acceptable." The auditor may or may not call attention to borderline interpretations of sales, valuation, or costs. But as we will see, there is no definitive standard.

Second, there are many cases in which one auditor may refuse to allow a questionable accounting practice to exist or to continue, but another auditor may be persuaded to allow that practice to fall within the limits of general acceptance. Because the auditors are retained and paid by the client companies, there is a constant pressure on the auditors to interpret these situations in the company's favor wherever possible. An auditor who exhibits excessive independence risks losing the client. The larger the client, the greater the pressure to "work with them."

The fact that financial statements from Enron, Global Crossing, Informix, and other companies did not present accurate pictures of financial results and condition is not disputed. The mischief is that only a small part, if any, of the company's behavior is likely to be illegal. Unethical and reprehensible perhaps, but not illegal.

The auditors are only human. It is likely that the laws will be strengthened in a futile attempt to compensate for that unfortunate condition. But regardless of the law, the real difficulty for you in a situation involving questionable accounting or fudging the numbers is this: If and when the situation blows up, no one will know whether you were one of the good guys, one of the miscreants, or one of the clueless. The very name of a tainted company on your resume will reduce or eliminate your chances for further consideration by a potential employer.

I Thought This Was a Math Book

Oh, it is a math book. More important, it's a book on math as a tool and a helper, not as a demon or an obstacle. Once you start thinking of math, accounting, and financial concepts as tools, you begin to realize that they are under human control and that they can help you.

In this introduction, I have tried to show you that math is not an unchanging granite temple but a tool that either you use or will be used against you. The caveat is that clarity will indeed cast a glaring light on performance, good or bad. Many people, perhaps some in your organization, would rather not have their activities explained too clearly; they profit from confusion and murkiness of information.

In the pages that follow, we look at record keeping, measurement, evaluation, and forecasting as these activities affect your performance and your future. It is a perspective not often seen, and too little understood. We also look at the math aspects of marketing's four P's: Product, Price, Place, and Promotion. Through it all, I will try to identify and explain realistic approaches to making math a tool that you use, rather than an instrument of torture that is used on you.

Two

Figures Never Lie, but Liars Figure

It's Absolute and Definite (Maybe), Part II

The old saying I borrowed to name this chapter accurately describes the use of accounting techniques in an organization, with one addition: People who aren't liars also figure.

We are observing a hiring situation. Three candidates apply for a position as chief financial officer (CFO). They are each asked the same question as part of the interview: "How much is 2 plus 2?"

Candidate A replies "4," and is told they'll get back to him.

Candidate B has studied statistics and knows the world is not exact. He replies, "Between 3.9 and 4.1; give me a moment and I'll calculate the standard deviation." They'll get back to him, too

Candidate C gets the job. His answer is, "How much do you want it to be?"

It's an old joke in the accounting profession, and I include it here for two reasons: (1) so you can say you heard it, if you hadn't heard it before and (2) to reinforce the idea that accounting's "reality" is a human perception, not an immutable law of nature or mathematics.

Is "Actual" Actually "Actual"?

Accounting involves two basic activities: (1) recording and evaluating the activity of the firm and (2) projecting or estimating what the future will hold. You might expect that predicting the future, or forecasting, is a less than exact science. What may be surprising to you is that recording and evaluating an organization's activities is not an exact science either. It may be a surprise to you, because the practitioners of those activities have tried to portray them as an exact science and have endlessly told us that they are. But because they are subject to human decisions, they are not. We'll take up the forecasting, estimating, and budgeting activities later on. Let's start here by taking a fresh look at the recording and evaluating function.

You may have the idea that in recording actual transactions and operating results, there is accuracy and objectivity; "actual," after all, means "actual," doesn't it?

Not necessarily. The application of different accounting techniques and formulas to the raw data from operations can yield different results from the same raw data. Those results may therefore be interpreted as more favorable or less favorable to different departments in the company. In many cases, there are winners and losers, depending on which alternate approach is taken. Wherever there might be "winners and losers," there will be people seeking to cast the data in a light favorable to themselves.

Take, as a simple example, a consulting firm or law firm. The time of the principals and associates is billed by the hour and allocated among the firm's various clients and projects through a system of time sheets, with job and task numbers. How is the time of senior members of the firm and the support staff allocated among the projects? The usual answer is that they are allocated in whatever manner the top management desires and decrees. Many junior project managers have encountered hours billed to their projects by senior people in the firm that the junior project managers can't recall having been spent.

By filling out their time sheets, senior managers have just (a) improved their own billable-time percentage (that is, increasing the portion of their expensive time billed to a client rather than being a deadweight cost to the firm) and (b) adversely affected the profit margin of that individual project. Why was the time billed to that project instead of others, or to "overhead"? Usually, because that project had some fat in it (i.e., it was more profitable than others) and because it was thought that the junior project managers, being junior, would be constrained by discretion or fear from squawking about it. The point here is that had those hours been allocated elsewhere, there would have been a different set of cost allocations, winners, and losers, based on the same raw data.

Another example: When is a sale a sale? This becomes a problem of timing. Many companies record a sale as having happened as of the moment the contract or sales order is signed or one nanosecond after the electronic transmission of the order is made. Why? Because it looks best for the company to have its sales recorded as soon as humanly possible; it boosts the sales figure on the Income Statement.

Notice that no effort has yet been made to fulfill that order, nothing has been shipped, and it's quite likely that no actual payments for the products ordered will be forthcoming for some time. But it has been decided that the sale will be recorded as of that date, in full. This can be particularly misleading when the contract is a large one, with many phases over a few years.

It might be more appropriate to spread the revenue out to approximate more closely the relationship between costs incurred and payments actually received. But no; it is a "generally accepted principle" that the entire sale can be noted while the ink is still wet on the contract. That makes us look good right now, when we need to look good. The most important accounting period is the current one.

So, accounting for a firm's operations is not an exact science. There are many choices underlying financial reporting, and these choices are made by people, after discussion and negotiation, for human reasons. As I noted, once they're approved by top management, they become reality.

Accounting Basics

Two very simple equations underlie every accounting system and process. They are

1. **Assets = Liabilities + Equity**

2. **Revenue – Costs = Profit**

The fundamental principle of accounting (upon which everybody does agree) is balance. Look at the first equation. It shows that our assets must equal, or balance out against, our liabilities plus our equity. In simple terms, that means that what we have equals what we owe plus what we own. If we own a house with a mortgage, the value of the house is what we have, the asset. The mortgage balance is what we owe, the liability. The difference between the mortgage balance and the value of the house is what we actually own, our equity. (And yes, equity can be a negative number, which would mean that we owe more than we have. Such a condition means inevitable misery in the future, if not in the present.)

Similarly, revenues or sales represent the money we take in, whereas costs or expenses represent the money we spend. Profit is what we have left. If we spend more than we take in, we have a loss. Losses are often printed in red ink. If we can't afford red ink (possibly because of the losses), we place the number in parentheses.

The Chart of Accounts

For each and every item of asset, liability, or equity, there is an account, or a recorded summary of transactions. This may be on paper or in a computer file. There is also an account for every category of income and expense.

Each organization has a list of all the accounts it uses; this is called the Chart of Accounts. There are Asset accounts, Liability accounts, and Equity accounts, and there are Revenue (Sales) accounts, and Expense accounts. I have provided a sample Chart of Accounts in Appendix B, but you should also take a look at your own firm's Chart of Accounts. Depending on the complexity of the business (and the fussiness of the accountants), that list or chart may contain less than a hundred or more than a thousand numbered accounts, covering all aspects of the firm's operations.

There is almost always a numbering system for these accounts. The most widely used system has accounts numbered with Asset accounts in the 100 or 1000 series, Liability accounts in the 200 or 2000 series, Equity accounts in the 300 or 3000 series, Revenue accounts in the 400 or 4000 series, and Expense accounts in the 500 or 5000 series.

Because of the way they are laid out on paper, these are often called T-accounts, with a left side and a right side.

If we look at our Balance Sheet equation again, the overall T-account would look like this:

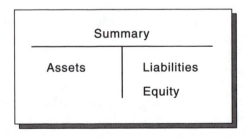

Figure 2.1   Basic T-Account

And because the total Assets on the left side of the ledger equal the sum of Liabilities and Equity on the right side of the ledger, the balance is zero.

Each and every account in the Chart of Accounts, regardless of whether it's an Asset, Expense, Liability, Equity, or Revenue account, looks like this:

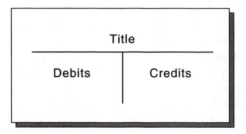

Figure 2.2   Account Format

Entries on the left side of the account are called debits, and entries on the right side of the account are called credits. The net difference between debits and credits is the balance, which, as I said, may be positive or negative.

Debits and Credits

At this point, you (along with thousands of other people) may be confused by the words *debit* and *credit*. To explain what accountants are talking about, we must try to remove the mystery from these two perfectly good words derived from Latin: *debitum*, to have owed, and *creditum*, a loan. The ancient common usage was to say that extension of credit increased a loan balance and that debits paid off the loan.

Many people have become confused about debits and credits because their lifelong understanding is that credits are good, because they increase your assets, and debits are bad, because they reduce your assets. Yet, as we will see, a debit increases asset accounts such as cash, which is a positive influence. How can that be?

Closer investigation shows that the common perception about debits and credits is the result of numerous notifications by your bank or by a company from which you buy things about "crediting your account," which means that you either have more or owe less, or "debiting your account," which means that you either have less or owe more.

The answer is not necessarily simple, but it becomes clearer if you remember that the bank or company is looking at the transaction from its point of view and its ledger, not yours. (To many who have dealt with banks, the idea that a bank would look at a transaction from its point of view instead of yours is not at all surprising.) The balance in your "account" on that bank's or company's books, which they are crediting or debiting, is in their eyes a liability account, on the right side of their ledger, meaning that they owe you that much money. The money in your account is a credit balance to them, and the higher your checkbook balance, the more money they owe you. If you make a $200 deposit in your checking account, the bank's liability to you increases by $200; they credit your account.

Hence, the public's common understanding is that the word *credit* is a good thing and the word *debit* is bad, meaning a reduction in your available money.

But, from your own perspective, cash is an asset. In your company's or your personal cash account, which is an asset account, you note that debits, being on the left, increase the cash balance, and credits decrease it.

A fable known to all accountants is the story of the CFO (chief financial officer) who retired after a long and distinguished career as an accountant. Over the years, his colleagues had noted that each morning, he would unlock the center drawer of his desk, consult a small card, nod, and replace the card. He would then relock the drawer. The staff was convinced that the card contained some kind of touchstone for their chief's success. His successor, going through the desk that was now his, opened the drawer and found the card, still there after years of use. Now he would know the secret that had served his predecessor so well. The card read, "The debits are the ones by the window, the credits are the ones by the door."

That means the window was on our hero's left, and the door was on his right. That's the usual format: debits on the left, credits on the right. (It may help you at this point to turn around so that in the room you're now in, the window is on the left and the door is on the right. Don't be embarrassed to do it; you'll be the only one who'll know why you did it.)

Figure 2.3 shows the relationship between the types of accounts. Think of zero as being in the middle, at the equal sign. Increases in accounts move the balances further from zero, to the left or right, and decreases move them closer to zero.

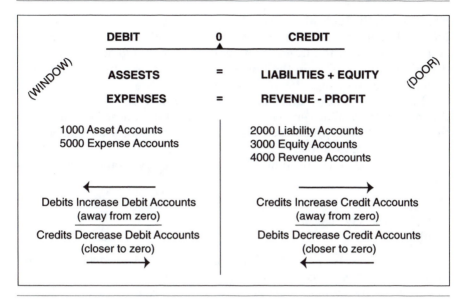

Figure 2.3   Debits, Credits, and Balance

Our two basic equations are also represented. The first is Assets = Liabilities + Equity. Assets (being on the left side of the equal sign, or near the window) are Debit accounts, and Liability and Equity accounts (being on the right side of the equal sign, or near the door) are Credit accounts.

Expense accounts are treated as Debit accounts, and Revenue accounts are on the credit side of the ledger. That means:

1. If you increase an Asset account or an Expense account, it's a debit. The increase is shown on the debit (left, or window) side of the ledger.

2. Conversely, if you decrease an Asset account or an Expense account, it's a credit (right side). Credits decrease Debit accounts.

3. And, if you increase a Liability, Equity, or Revenue account, it's a credit. The increase shows on the credit (right, or door) side.

4. If you decrease a Liability, Equity, or Revenue account, it's a debit (left side).

Of such convolutions are accounting careers made.

Journals and Double Entry

The process that ensures balance for all accounts is this: Every time you make a debit entry in an account, there must be an equal, corresponding, offsetting credit entry in some other account. Every transaction is listed as it is made in the Journal, or Daily Journal. Every transaction listed in the Journal has its debit and credit entries, showing the amounts and the accounts to which the transactions will be posted. Obviously, the total debits and total credits in the Journal for each day's activities must also match, that is, they must be in balance.

The account entries must be made in pairs, a lockstep that keeps things in balance. Once entered in the Journal, the transaction entries are then posted to the proper accounts. Track this process by referring to Appendix B. For example:

We buy $200 worth of lumber. The Journal entry would show in this format:

Account	Debit	Credit
1200 Inventory-Lumber	200	
1012 Cash		200

We have increased the Asset account for lumber by debiting it and decreased the Asset account for cash by crediting it.

If you borrow money from the bank, you receive the cash and add it to the Cash Asset account by debiting. The Liability account, Notes Payable-Bank, goes up by $1,000, which you show by a credit.

Account	Debit	Credit
1012 Cash	1,000	
2020 Notes Payable-Bank		1,000

If you pay off part of a loan, you reduce (credit) your Cash (Asset) account and reduce (debit) your loan (Liability) account. In the Journal, the double entry looks like this:

Account	Debit	Credit
2020 Notes Payable-Bank	1,000	
1012 Cash		1,000

A more complicated entry might involve purchasing two different items from the same supplier at the same time, say, some wood that will go into your product and some lubricating oil for your machinery. Here are the Journal entries to the accounts involved:

Account	Debit	Credit
1200 Inventory-Lumber	500	
5451 Oils and Lubricants	200	
1012 Cash		700

Notice that the total of the debits for the transaction must equal the total of the credits for the transaction. When you hear accountants gnashing their teeth about the books "not balancing," they are looking for either a calculation error or part of a double-entry transaction that somehow got posted to the wrong account.

The Two-Phase Transaction

Sometimes it takes two steps, perhaps days or weeks apart, to complete a transaction. The best example is the purchase of lumber that we used before. But instead of paying cash, we make a credit purchase, to be paid later. The Journal entry for Step 1 resembles the cash purchase, but there's a crucial difference:

Account		Debit	Credit
1200	Inventory-Lumber	200	
2010	Accounts Payable		200

We have increased the Lumber account (1200) as before, but instead of decreasing cash, we have increased our Accounts Payable account. Remember, a credit increases Liability accounts. But, we still have one debit and an equal, offsetting credit. When we do pay the bill, the transaction will look like this:

Account		Debit	Credit
2010	Accounts Payable	200	
1012	Cash		200

We reduce the liability through a debit and reduce cash with a credit. The system remains in balance whether we're dealing with the left side of the ledger, the right side of the ledger, or both sides.

One major advantage of double-entry bookkeeping systems is that they provide a framework for discovering errors and mishandled transactions easily. The Journal must always be in balance, and the balances in the Debit (left side) accounts must equal the balances in the Credit (right side) accounts. This also creates less opportunity for embezzlement or other kinds of theft by a dishonest employee.

Sales and Expenses

Double-entry bookkeeping also explains why sales and expenses are treated in a way that seems confusing.

Notice that in our last Journal example above, one of the accounts debited was an Asset account and the other account was an Expense account.

This should help to explain why both Asset and Expense accounts are treated as Debit or left-side accounts. We'll look at that in just a moment. Right now, consider this: If cash goes down, either assets or expenses are going to go up. Alternately, in transactions involving accounts on both sides of the ledger, if cash goes down, either liabilities or equity will also go down because we have paid off all or part of a loan or paid a dividend to our owners.

We said that the Revenue (400 or 4000 series) and Expenses (500 or 5000 series) accounts are summarized in the Income Statement and that the equation here is stated as

$$\text{Revenue} - \text{Costs} = \text{Profit}$$

Put another way, what we receive, less what we spend, equals what we keep. Obviously, if we spend more than we receive during a given period, we have a negative profit, or a loss for that period. Losses are not evil in themselves; we sometimes plan for a short-term loss, calling it an "investment," in order to fund a project that will lead to a long-term profit. What is bad is an unplanned loss, a loss that doesn't result in the anticipated long-term profit or a loss that goes on for a longer time than had been forecast.

The confusion comes about because the Revenue accounts are Credit or right-side accounts and are treated like Equity accounts, that is, a credit increases them. The Expense accounts, remember, are treated the same as Asset accounts, that is, a debit increases them. Why? Why treat an expense like an asset and a sale like a liability? The accountants have a long list of explanations for this, which all boil down to, "It's easier for the accountants to do it that way." It's not revealed science; the system was set up deliberately so that the sacred balance of debits and credits would be maintained.

It goes back to double entry. Accountants set the chart up so that, for example, when a cash sale is made, they credit Revenue and debit or increase Cash (Asset). When they buy raw material, they credit (decrease) Cash and debit (increase) Materials Inventory (Asset). When they pay for repair of a machine by a contractor, they credit Cash (Asset) and debit Repair Expense (Expense).

When goods or services are sold to a customer on a Cash Basis, we increase (debit) Cash and increase (credit) that customer's Revenue account.

Let's oversimplify things just a bit here. When a Revenue (or Sales) account (credit) increases, we get money, so cash increases (debit cash). When an Expense account (debit) increases, we have spent money, so cash decreases (credit cash).

The Revenue and Expense accounts are designed to be temporary. At the end of each specified period (usually each month), the accountants "close out" these accounts. That means they look at each Revenue and Expense account and add up all the Revenue and Expense account balances in that period. The net difference between the Revenue account total and the Expense account total represents the profit or loss for that period, which becomes the profit account. They then set up new Revenue and Expense accounts, with zero balances, for the next period.

This system makes Profit a Credit account, just like Equity. If there is a positive profit, it's a credit, which translates to an increase in the value of what we own. It keeps everything neat. If it confuses the nonaccountants, well, that's just another reason to have accountants. Or for you to learn a bit about accounting, which is what you're doing.

Revenue, Sales, and Income

I have called the 4000-series accounts Revenue accounts. Some companies call them Sales accounts and others call them Income accounts, which could be sources of further confusion. *Revenue* is the all-encompassing term.

There are other sources of revenue besides sales; for example, service fees or earned interest. But the most confusion arises out of the term *income*.

We often think of "all the money we receive" as income. After all, we pay an "income tax" on our personal incomes, much adjusted. But managers and accountants also use the term *income* as a synonym for *profit* to describe what part of their revenues they have left after some or all of their expenses. So, when you hear someone say "income," stop and check out whether that person is describing revenue or profit. There is a large and vital difference.

It's an Accrual, Accrual World

Now that we have debits, credits, revenue, and income straight, let's look at another word that confuses many people: *accrual*.

Basically, there are two ways to keep track of what's going on in an organization. We can keep track of cash in and cash out, recording receipts and payments as they happen. That's called accounting on a Cash Basis.

The problem with the Cash Basis is that it doesn't accurately reflect the impact of things paid for in advance or not paid for until later. Let's assume that a company keeps track of its revenues and costs and issues a financial statement each month. If, for example, we pay a $1,200 annual insurance premium in July, that puts a rather large hole in our July financial result. The next 11 months would be untouched, and our costs would look lower than they actually are.

But insurance doesn't work that way; it runs at a level rate all year long. To be as accurate as possible, we should allocate $100, or $1/12$ of the premium, to each of the 12 months in the year. If we do that, showing a $100 insurance cost in each month's expense statement, we are said to accrue the monthly expense over the applicable period, regardless of the month in which we physically write the annual check and reduce (credit) our cash balance.

Thus, the accrual system of accounting allocates costs to the periods in which they are actually incurred rather than when they're paid for. Although the accrual system provides more accurate information, it also provides much employment for accountants. More important, you should recognize that there are many possible methods of accrual allocation, and they are all within human control.

Let us now turn to the method by which financial information is summarized for presentation to managers, stockholders, bankers, and other interested parties.

Three

Making a (Financial) Statement

How Are We Doing?

All the accounts in the Chart of Accounts, regardless of how many there are, can be (and must be) summarized into the basic formatted statements that we are about to study. The idea is to present information that will show (in the best possible light) how the firm is performing under its noble and enlightened managers (especially if that's us).

At a given time, usually 5:00 p.m. on the last working day of an accounting period, the books are closed. That is, the transactions relating to that period are summarized and totaled, and those numbers are transferred to financial statements. The accounting period can be a month, a quarter, a year, or whatever period is determined by the board of directors.

Generally speaking, the Asset, Liability, and Equity account (100, 200, and 300) balances are transferred to a Balance Sheet, and the Sales and Expense account (400 and 500) balances are transferred to an Income Statement. The formats and legal rules for such statements are more rigid and more consistent now that they have been in previous years, particularly for publicly held companies.

You may think that the tax laws have forced companies to be more consistent in their financial reporting, but it ain't necessarily so. Oh, they're consistent from year to year, but most companies file tax returns that look considerably different from the reports they issue to stockholders. There is nothing wrong with that; it's done because tax considerations (called loopholes by those who can't profit from them) often cause accounting allocations that, if followed without deviation, would present an inaccurate picture of the operation to the stockholders. (Remember, the company wants to look less profitable to the tax collector but more profitable to its stockholders.)

Yes, that sounds like keeping two sets of books. But keeping two sets of books is neither illegal nor unusual. Actually, there's only one set of basic books or computer files with the Daily Journal and the accounts. What's different is the way information is extracted from that database and summarized for different purposes.

The Balance Sheet

The company-wide summary of the Assets = Liabilities + Equity situation as of a specific point in time is called a Balance Sheet, although it is more formally called a Statement of Condition.

Figure 3.1 is a simple Balance Sheet for a hypothetical firm, the Bilgewater Beverage Company. It shows the standard format. We're going to look at this thing line by line. Before we do that, however, let's ask a question: Can we tell from a Balance Sheet how a company is doing? Whether or not it's making money? No, we can't.

A Balance Sheet is a statement of condition, not a statement of performance. Remember, a Balance Sheet shows the financial condition of the firm as of a certain date and time (usually the close of business on the date of issue). If you look at two of the firm's Balance Sheets from successive dates, you can make some inferences, but you still can't get an accurate picture of performance from only the Balance Sheets. That comes from the Income Statement, of which more anon.

Now let's look at each of the line items in the Balance Sheet.

Assets

Current Assets: those assets that can quickly be turned into cash; often called liquid assets, because liquids flow more easily than solids. Some of these accounting definitions can be unexpectedly vivid, can't they?

Cash: Bilgewater's bank balances, or cash equivalents.

Accounts Receivable: the amount that Bilgewater's customers have been invoiced for and have not yet paid. Some of this may be past due. Most of it is just normal trade credit, within a normal billing cycle.

Bilgewater Beverage Company
Statement of Condition
December 31, 2004   *(Balance Sheet)*

ASSETS

Current Assets

Cash	$ 400,000	
Accounts receivable	550,000	
Notes receivable	300,000	
Inventory	220,000	
Prepaid expenses	50,000	
Total Current Assets		$ 1,520,000

Fixed Assets

Land		900,000
Factory	6,500,000	
Manufacturing equipment	2,200,000	
Total	8,700,000	
Less accumulated depreciation	3,900,000	
Net Total Plant & Equipment		4,800,000
Investments		600,000
Other Fixed Assets		100,000
Total Fixed Assets		6,400,000
Total Assets		$ 7,920,000

LIABILITIES

Current Liabilities

Accounts payable	$ 290,000	
Notes payable	230,000	
Total current liabilities		$ 520,000

Fixed Liabilities

Mortgage payable	1,100,000	
Total fixed liabilities		1,100,000
Total Liabilities		$ 1,620,000

EQUITY

Common Stock, par value	4,000,000	
Retained Earnings	2,300,000	
Total Equity		$ 6,300,000
Total Liabilities and Equity		$ 7,920,000

Figure 3.1   Sample Balance Sheet

Notes Receivable: amounts due to be paid to Bilgewater from sources other than their customer accounts. Usually used to show short-term investments by Bilgewater.

Inventory: the value (at cost or market value, and not the assumed sales price or hoped for sales value) of the products Bilgewater sells, and materials that go into the products, that are on hand as of the Balance Sheet date.

Prepaid Expenses: things that Bilgewater has paid for in advance, for example, the unexpired portion of an annual insurance policy.

Fixed Assets: those assets that cannot quickly be turned into cash; our "permanent" facilities.

Factory: the cost (or market value) of Bilgewater's building, which they own.

Manufacturing Equipment: the cost (or market value) of the tools and equipment Bilgewater owns for production.

Accumulated Depreciation: the total, so far, of the annual deductions from the total cost of fixed assets made to account for wear and tear over the equipment's lifetime. If it helps you to think of this as an annual use fee for equipment they bought some time ago, please do. Accumulated depreciation is subtracted from the asset's original value to arrive at a net value of the assets. The theory is that at the end of each asset's useful life, accumulated depreciation will equal most of the original asset value, leaving only the scrap value of the asset on the books.

Investments: the cost of investments made by the company. This could be stocks, bonds, diamonds, anything in which the company may legally invest.

Other Fixed Assets: a miscellaneous category for items such as incorporation and trademark costs added to capital rather than treated as expense items.

Liabilities

Current Liabilities: what Bilgewater owes to its creditors that must be paid within this next year. The whole concept of "current" versus "fixed" has to do with whether the asset is paid for in this year or later than that over a number of years.

Accounts Payable: what Bilgewater owes its suppliers. It is presumed that the suppliers' invoices will be paid in less than a year. At least, the suppliers definitely have that presumption.

Fixed Liabilities: what Bilgewater owes that is payable after this current year.

Mortgage Payable: what Bilgewater owes that it will have to pay more than a year from now. (The part of the mortgage that Bilgewater owes this year is a current liability.)

Equity

Common Stock: the par value of the company's Common stock, which, in general, is the money Bilgewater received when the stock was first issued. This has nothing to do with the current price of the shares if they are traded

Retained Earnings: accumulated profits (earnings) that have not (yet) been distributed to stockholders. This figure has no relationship to last year's (or any year's) profits. It also is not a fudged number that was inserted just to make things balance

The Income Statement

The Income Statement is a report of the results of the company's operations during a stated time period (not a point in time). The most common analogy is that the Balance Sheet is a snapshot, a still photo of the institution's condition at a point in time, whereas the Income Statement is the movie recording activity during a certain period of time.

Like the Balance Sheet, the Income Statement also follows a standardized formula. It is a summary of all the Sales and Expense accounts contained in the Chart of Accounts. Figure 3.2 is a sample Income Statement; we'll take a look at each line item.

Gross Sales: the total of all valid invoices Bilgewater sent out during the year.

Returns and Allowances: deductions made from sales because the customers never paid these amounts. An item may have been returned and money refunded, or a product may have been slightly damaged and a negotiated reduction in payment was allowed to compensate for the customer's inconvenience and receipt of a "lesser" product. These are listed as adjustments to sales rather than as expenses, because Bilgewater never got the money.

Discounts: deductions from sales because discounts were allowed.

Total Adjustments to Sales: the sum of allowances and discounts, subtracted from gross sales. A high number here, relative to total sales, is a danger sign, because it indicates that somebody may have gotten carried away with unrealistic sales.

In fact, every marketing person must pay close attention to the difference between gross sales and net sales, all the time. Every item that reduces gross sales represents some degree of dissatisfaction by one or more customers. The operating statement should be viewed as an early warning system. Check out the details of returns and allowances by product, by geographic area, and by customer; look for patterns or activity. Is it shipping damage? Is it customers believing they were misled? Is it a defective product or component? Is it poor follow-up?

Bilgewater Beverage Company (Profit & Loss)
Income Statement
For the year ending December 31, 2004

Gross Sales		$7,360,000	
Less returns and allowances	130,000		104.40%
Less discounts	180,000		
Total Adjustments to Sales:		310,000	4.40%
Net Sales		7,050,000	100.00%
Other Income		260,000	
TOTAL REVENUE		7,310,000	
Cost of Goods Sold			
Inventory, January 1, 2004		440,000	6.24%
Purchases	1,600,000		22.7%
Freight in	60,000		0.85%
Cost of purchases	1,600,000		23.55%
Added labor	1,400,000		19.86%
Other direct costs	300,000		4.26%
Goods available for sale	3,800,00		53.90%
Less inventory, December 31, 2004	220,000		3.12%
Costs of goods sold		3,580,000	50.78%
Gross Profit From Sales (Gross Margin)		3,730,000	52.91%
Operating expenses			
Sales expense	630,000		8.94%
Advertising expense	240,000		3.40%
General salaries	1,350,00		19.15%
Supplies	40,000		0.57%
Depreciation	320,00		4.54%
Insurance, fees	50,000		0.71%
Other	70,000		0.99%
Total Operating Expenses		2,700,000	38.30%
NET INCOME BEFORE TAXES		1,030,000	14.61%
Income Tax Expense		670,000	9.50%
Net Income (after taxes)		360,000	5.11%

Figure 3.2   Sample Income Statement

Net Sales: the dollar value assigned to the stuff that was sold and stayed sold, which is the "real" sales figure.

Cost of Goods Sold: a calculated number that identifies the direct costs of acquiring and manufacturing the items that Bilgewater sold. The calculation "backs into" the cost of what was sold this way: We begin with

Inventory, January 1, 2004: what we had on hand at the beginning of the year. All inventory is required to be valued at its cost or the market value, whichever is lower. It is not valued at the sale price, which has no relationship to costs.

Purchases: the dollar value of all the goods and materials that Bilgewater bought during the year to go into its products. Any discounts or allowances Bilgewater got are included in this number.

Freight In: the cost of getting the goods from the supplier to Bilgewater.

Cost of Purchases: the total of purchases of goods for sale, plus freight in.

Added Labor: the cost of paying our employees who modify and assemble the materials and goods that come in, in order to produce the company's product. Often called "adding value."

Goods Available for Sale: our calculation of the Cost of Goods Sold next adds the cost of what Bilgewater had at the beginning of the year to the cost of the goods purchased during the year. By doing that, we obtain the cost of all the goods that Bilgewater might have sold during the year. If their end-of-year inventory were zero, then the cost of goods available for sale would be the cost of the goods that were sold. They would all be gone. But,

Inventory, December 31, 2004: it isn't zero. It hardly ever is zero. So, we must subtract the dollar value of the inventory Bilgewater has on hand at the end of the year from the dollar value of everything they had available for sale, because they didn't sell it all. Cost of Goods Sold is the cost of what they did sell, because they no longer have it in inventory.

At this point, somebody usually asks, "Hey, what if some of those goods or materials not in the ending inventory were stolen or destroyed instead of being sold?" The answer is, If it's not there, and it still cost us money, it's part of our Cost of Goods Sold, no matter how it disappeared. It's still a cost.

To repeat: The calculation for *Cost of Goods Sold* is

> Beginning Inventory (what we started with)
> Plus Purchases (what we bought or added during the period)
>   and added labor;
> Minus Ending Inventory (what we had left or did not sell)

Now we subtract the Cost of Goods Sold we have just calculated from the Net Sales to arrive at the *Gross Profit from Sales* (*Gross Margin*).

But that's only half the story. There are also expenses that don't directly relate to the acquisition and/or manufacture of our product but rather relate more generally to the running of the business. For example, the executive and office salaries are more or less fixed for the year; they are not normally determined by multiplying some factor by the number of items produced. For example, Bilgewater's mortgage is the same regardless of how many bottles (or gallons) of beverages move off the loading dock. The total of these expenses must be subtracted from the gross profit to arrive at

Net Profit (before taxes)

Next, we subtract

Income Tax expense, to arrive at
Net Income (after taxes).

This last line, Net Income, is the last line at the bottom of the Income Statement. That's why it's often called "the bottom line." The idea is that this dollar number should be as much above zero as possible. The Net Income figure is also the best measure of (a) how well we have satisfied our customers and (b) how effectively we have used the resources allocated to us.

Note that in many organizations, the number used to judge the operations of the company is Net Income Before Taxes, because we do not control the tax rate.

Fiscal Years

We have all heard the term *fiscal year*. Some people think it's a "physical" year. But it usually only gets physical after it goes sour.

No, a fiscal year is nothing more than an arbitrary 12-month period selected for accounting purposes. It could coincide with the calendar year, but it doesn't have to. The U.S. federal government, for example, used to have a fiscal year that began on July 1 and ended on June 30. Many states, public institutions, and companies followed that lead. A few years ago, faced with delays in getting a budget prepared, Congress passed a law moving the federal fiscal year to begin on October 1 and end on September 30. Most states and other institutions and companies did not follow suit.

If you want to have some fun at work, try asking the accountants and other people, "Why do we have the fiscal year we have?" The chances are that you'll hear some variation on the theme "That's the way it's always been."

But the thing for you to remember is that the fiscal year was not handed down from on high for the ages. There's no magic about a fiscal year; it was selected by people. The question is, Was it selected with the conditions of your business in mind?

Quite often, a fiscal year is selected for the convenience of the accountants, rather than the best interest of the business. The closing and cutoff dates are all-important; the main focus is on the paperwork and on consistency.

Consider Companies A and B, both of which have their peak sales period in the fourth calendar quarter, particularly the Christmas season. The first three quarters are lackluster, complete with an even slower summer season.

Company A uses the calendar year as its fiscal year. Costs occur all year, including costs of preparing for Christmas. The costs are close to or greater than revenues until the fourth quarter, the peak sales period. So the company may show a loss for 9 months, then appear to bounce back in the magic fourth quarter. A major drawback is that until almost to the end of the year, annual totals are uncertain because a major activity period (namely, the period of greatest revenue) is unresolved.

Company B, otherwise identical to Company A, uses a fiscal year that begins October 1. The first quarter statement shows the Christmas sales and the fourth quarter costs. The remaining 9 months will involve a slower profit growth, or even a shrinking annual profit figure, but the year will look much better overall. It will also be a clearer picture, because the items that have the greatest impact on the financial statement will be known earlier in the fiscal year, well before the final accounting period. Uncertainty exists for a shorter period of time, which also improves the mental health of the management.

In general, then, the ideal fiscal year should begin just before your greatest period of customer activity and revenue, just before your busy season. There's no law of physics that says it can't.

Every once in a while, some corporate planners get carried away and try to compensate for the unevenness of the Gregorian calendar. A few years ago, one major corporation in the United States "streamlined" its accounting by establishing a 52-week fiscal year, beginning on the first Monday in January, which wasn't January 1st. As you might expect, in a few years, the leftover days had added up. Yes, we were all treated to the inevitable 53-week fiscal year when the adjustment was made. Making the adjustments caused more confusion and work than the "simplification" allegedly saved.

Another genius noted that weekly reporting periods were too short and monthly reporting periods too long. And they were uneven because of holidays. He figured that there were about 113 weekend days and holidays in the calendar year. This left 252 workdays in the year. Those 252 days divided exactly into thirty-six 7-workday periods, which would make things come out even. You guessed it—the new reporting periods were to end 7 workdays apart, regardless of intervening weekends or holidays. For a year that started with January 1 as a Monday, Period 1 ended on the second Wednesday in January (remember, January 1 was a holiday). Period 2 ended 7 workdays later, on the third Friday. Period 3 ended on the fifth Tuesday. By Period 4, which was to end on the second Thursday in February, everybody was hopelessly lost. The shiny new system disappeared under the weight of untranslated weekly reports, miscalculations of dates, requests for clarification, blistering complaint memos, and no reports at all. The CFO took (or was pushed into) early retirement, saying as he went, "But it was all so simple, and everything worked out evenly!"

Moral: Try to make the calendar work for you, rather than you working for the calendar.

Four

Organizations, Measurement, and Standards

How Are You Doing?

We have looked at the two basic reporting statements that are common to all organizations: the Balance Sheet and the Income Statement. There is no easy way to say this: If you are to be successful, you must understand them; you cannot escape. Take a closer look at the statements for your company or organization. Look at the similarities and differences between your statements and my samples.

These are the basics. The remainder of this book will peel away the next layer and look at some of the concepts that underlie how the items on those statements got to be what they are. I'll also give you a better understanding of the numbers upon which you will be judged.

What Are We, Anyway?

The type of organization with which we are involved will have a bearing on how the financial structure will be set up and on how we are judged.

A very basic point is that there are three types of formal and legal organizational structures: sole proprietorship, partnership, and corporation.

In a sole proprietorship, one person owns the company. Period. That person is the boss and the final authority. The sole proprietor is also faced with something called unlimited liability, that is, sole proprietors are liable for any debts of the business to the extent of all of their personal resources, and perhaps more. Sole proprietors are responsible only to creditors and to the tax collectors; there are no stockholders. That means there are no public financial reporting requirements, and it is quite likely that the accounting system is relatively informal. If you work for a sole proprietor, you are indeed working for an individual, not an organized entity or group.

Where more than one person owns a business, we quite often see the partnership form of organization used. In a partnership, a group of people agree to share the investment in and profits from the organization's operations. There is (or should be) a formal partnership agreement, a document spelling out the shares of ownership, shares of profit, and responsibilities of the partners. With regard to liability, the general partners all have unlimited liability, just as sole proprietors do. There may be provisions for limited liability for investing partners who take no role in management, but the general rule is that partners are liable as if they were sole proprietors. Furthermore, a partnership is not subject to income tax as an entity. Tax on the income that flows to each partner must be paid by that partner.

The corporation form of ownership differs from sole proprietorships and partnerships in that a separate legal entity is created. That corporate entity is recognized as a "fictitious person" under the law. It is also taxed as if it were a separate person. The benefit is that liability of the shareholders is limited to the amount of their investment.

The shareholders in a corporation are the owners. More precisely, in most cases it is the holders of a majority of the Common stock shares who control the corporation. This is because it is usually only the Common shares that have voting rights. A corporation may issue Preferred stock with a prior claim on dividends, but Preferred shares usually carry no vote.

The voting shareholders exercise their ownership rights by electing a board of directors to govern the corporation. The full scope of the board's powers are set forth in the Articles of Incorporation and the By-laws of the corporation. The board hires and fires the CEO and other corporate officers.

But the formal organization is only part of the story. In practice, the corporate form is often adopted by single owners to limit their liability.

That person may own 99% of the Common stock, with a spouse or other relative holding only enough shares to qualify them for membership on the board of directors. Similarly, a group of partners may form a corporation but operate it like a partnership. The organizational form is less important than the relationships between the people in charge: the owners. They are the ultimate evaluators of performance of the organization and its people. Although there are common factors and "generally accepted principles," each organization is unique in its evaluation process and in what it considers to be important.

Different Purposes, Different Rulers

We have been looking at how accountants measure things, that is, transactions being recorded in separate accounts, which are classified and summarized periodically to report the results of operations and the condition of the organization. Note that the more accounts there are, the more detailed the accounting system and the greater the potential for precision. Unfortunately, that precision comes with a price: increased complexity. And as we shall see, precision is not the same thing as and does not necessarily lead to accuracy.

The recording and summarizing process gets us to profit and loss and to assets, liabilities, and equity. As I have already noted, the management decisions made about what will be measured, and how, will bias the information about which decisions will be made.

As opposed to accountants, financial people have a different approach to measurement. They take the data that the accountants present and analyze it to see how things are really going.

A Few Examples

Example 1: The Current Ratio

This is a simple measurement to see if the company owes too much for its own good. The finance person looks at the current assets and divides them by the current liabilities. Take Bilgewater Beverage. The Balance Sheet (see Figure 3.1) shows Current Assets totaling $1,520,000 versus Total Current Liabilities of $520,000. Even without a calculator, we can see that's almost a 3:1 ratio; that is, current assets total about three times as much as current liabilities. Generally, in the United States, 2:1 is considered OK in most situations; 1.5:1 is borderline. So, at more than 3:1, Bilgewater is in the comfortable range. In some countries, 3:1 is the safe point. The rule of thumb depends on whose thumb is on the document.

Oh, how did I do that without a calculator? Simple. I rounded off the numbers in my head, in this case to $1,500,000 and $500,000. So it's about 3:1. From there, I can make an estimate that is usually as close as we need to get. The calculator yields a ratio of 2.9230769:1 wretched excess.

By the way, this business of making a rough estimate in your head can have an interesting effect on your colleagues. While they reach for their calculators, you round off and estimate as we just described. Then you say, "That's a little less than 3 to1; not bad." Ten seconds later, they come up with the electronically assisted multidecimal answer, look up at you, and say, with a bit of wonder in their voices, "You're right!" Of course, you're right. Don't show them this book.

Example 2: Return on Assets (ROA)

This calculation involves dividing Net Profit by the assets invested in the enterprise. For Bilgewater, the Balance Sheet shows Total Assets of $7,920,000 and the Income Statement (see Figure 3.2) shows a Pretax Net Income Before Taxes of $1,030,000. That's about 15%. (Oh, all right, 14.61%.) Whether that's good or bad depends on the history, the norm for the industry, the economic climate, and so on. Actually, whether it's good or bad will be a subjective judgment of those in charge, depending on what they think is good or bad.

Example 3: Return on Equity (ROE)

This time we divide that $1,030,000 net profit by the $6,300,000 shown on the Balance Sheet as Total Equity. In a sense, that is what the stockholders have really invested, because they do owe that $1,620,000 liability (and they made a greater profit because of the money they borrowed). The figure of $1,030,000 divided by $6,300,000 is just over 16% (16.3492, to be excessively precise). Is that good? Bad? Well, that depends on the comparison. If you compare Company A's ROA with Company B's ROE, you'll get nothing meaningful.

The point of this is that reasonable people may legally differ over methods in the course of judging a company's performance. Or a manager's performance. If you don't take the time to make sure that the comparisons are made on a valid basis, you can't expect your competitors, however friendly, to do it for you.

A problem here is the very common use of the term *return on investment* (ROI). ROI has been used to describe both ROA and ROE; it's not precise. Make sure whenever ROI is being discussed that all parties know whether you're talking about ROA or ROE.

Example 4: Percentage of Sales

Many organizations compare almost every other number on the Income Statement to sales. These percentages provide a convenient rule of thumb to many managers. Two examples from Bilgewater: Gross Margin is 52.91% of Sales; Pretax Net Profit is 14.61% of Sales. (I used Net Sales here; it could have been Gross Sales. The important thing is that you know which one, choose it, and stick with it.)

There are many other percentages and ratios that financial people develop for comparison purposes. Most of them are beyond the scope of this book, but all of them use the same procedures. The main thing is that you understand the general process.

Percentage of What?

One aspect of using percentages for comparison can be overlooked: it's careful identification of the base number on which the comparison is made. Take, for example, a company that had sales of $800,000 last year and $880,000 in sales this year. We take the difference of $80,000 and divide it by—which number? Well, we're trying to track a change over time, so we use the earlier number, or $800,000. Thankfully, that makes the difference an even 10%.

So far, so good. But let's say that we're comparing the sales of two companies. Company A is $300,000 and Company B is $400,000. Well, that $100,000 difference can be 33.3% of Company A or 25% of Company B. Which base number is chosen will bias the interpretation of the difference: "a whopping" 33.3% or "only" 25%. The thing to make sure of is to use the same base for all comparisons. In other words, in the example above, pick Company A or Company B and stick with it.

We sometimes see comparisons made in which one figure is a percentage of sales and another a percentage of costs, or one figure is a percentage of Gross Sales and another a percentage of Net Sales. You can see how these could be misleading. Of course, no one would ever do that to spice up a presentation, would they? Of course not.

Another percentage problem causes trouble. I'll call it "much ado about very little."

"Do you realize that Johnson overshot some of his costs by 20%?" Sounds bad, until you learn that the cost item involved was a cab ride that cost $6 instead of $5. As you look at percentage comparisons, remember that the magnitude of an item is as important as the percentage. Johnson, by the way, was also 2% under budget on labor costs, and that budget item was $250,000. See the difference?

The Pitfalls of Precision

In the preceding sections, we have also been exposed to a subtle but important concept that any good manager masters: the concept of Appropriate Precision. I've already noted that we don't always need to calculate numbers out to seven places, and that many times, we can make an approximation in our heads. In the current ratio example shown above (Example 1), it didn't make any difference whether Bilgewater's actual current ratio was 3.0, 2.9, or 2.92307. For our purposes, just being up near 3.0 was very good.

A magazine ad costs you $2,132 and promises a circulation of 180,000 readers. Different magazines charge different rates and have different size readerships. The calculation that allows you to compare the magazines on a level basis is based on the cost per impression. We take each magazine's dollar ad rate and divide it by the readership. In doing this, we usually state the audience in thousands of impressions to get away from small decimals. We call that calculation the cost per thousand (CPM).

So, in this example, we divide $2,132 by 180. Right away we can see that it's a bit more than $10 per 1,000, or probably somewhere between $11 and $12. If we need to get closer, whip out the trusty calculator: $11.8444.

The only reason we see so many calculations made to many decimal places is that the calculator has enabled us to do so. But there is another more insidious aspect to this calculator-induced precision. It's called the Illusion of Accuracy. When we read that the probability of a customer choosing our product over that of Competitor A is 54.15261%, we're more likely, as human beings, to accept that number as accurate than if it was stated as "just over 50%." Those precise decimals make the number look much more scientific, don't they? And yet the measurement may have been sloppy, the assumptions flawed, the sample biased—all things that render the number less meaningful. But it looks precise.

Remember this: Precision and accuracy are not the same thing. Remember this particularly the next time you're listening to the Quality Control people recount their latest successes.

Why Are We Looking Here?

Another story, if I may.

A patrolman on a walking beat on a Saturday evening encounters a citizen on his hands and knees, looking for something on the sidewalk.

"Whatcha looking for, buddy?" asks the officer.

"I . . . I . . ." (the citizen has apparently overindulged in alcoholic pleasures). "I'm looking for a quarter I losht."

"OK," says the bemused cop, "Where did you lose it?"

"About a haffablock that way."

"Waidaminit! If you lost the quarter a half a block that way, why are you looking here?"

Triumphantly the citizen answers, "The lightsh better here!"

Yes, it seems silly, but we do it all the time. We tend to measure the things that are easy to measure rather than the things that are more relevant but not as easy to measure. For example, the number of people reached by an advertisement rather than the number of people in our target market reached, the number of hits on an Internet Web site rather than favorable experiences or resulting sales, the number of arrests rather than the number of people pointed away from crime, the number of students promoted rather than the number of students who can actually read.

My favorite example involves a state unemployment agency system that measures its performance by counting the number of unemployment applications filed. Now, if pressed, they will agree that the real measure of the state unemployment agency's effectiveness is the number of people actually placed in jobs. But that doesn't happen right away, it's complicated, and so forth. The easy thing to measure is applications, and that's what they measure.

The Unseen Costs of Saving Money

Another case: How do we judge the effectiveness of a company's product delivery system? The folks who move goods from the factory's outbound loading platform toward our customers do a daily job that is often taken for granted. All too often, their performance is judged by the number of products delivered versus the total dollars spent on delivery. Easy to measure. Get that average cost-per-shipment down.

But does cutting those shipping costs mean that a larger percentage of our customers are being inconvenienced by lengthened delivery times? We can save X easily measured dollars by going from 1-day to 2-day delivery; but how many dollars will be lost from customers who were inconvenienced by our cost cutting? Not as easy to measure; and besides, that's the problem of the Customer Service Department, not Transportation.

A well-known telephone company decided that its operator assistance calls could stand an improvement in efficiency. So, they applied pressure to their operators to not waste time but to get calls completed in 30 seconds or less. The measurement was time per call, which the switchboard electronics easily calculated. Success was measured in terms of fewer seconds per call, not how many people were actually assisted. The result was that fewer people actually got all the help they needed before being shuffled off the line by harried operators with one eye on an egg timer, trying to avoid the inevitable reprimand. The costs of frustrated customers (and the second calls made to clarify the first calls) were harder to identify.

There are too many customer-insensitive stories of this kind. They have as a common starting point some easily measured unit of productivity that "obviously" could and should be "improved upon." But you'll do a better job of marketing if you first ask, "Are we measuring the right thing?"

When certain numbers alone become the focus of measurement, some interesting unintended consequences can result. Salespeople are often measured, and compensated, in terms of Gross Sales quotas. Volume. Dollars To Us! Hit that Line! Sell!

The focus is on Gross Sales, because that's the figure on which commissions and bonuses are based. But is our strategy to improve Gross Sales or to improve profit? In too many cases, the salespeople have built volume by selling many of the least profitable items in the company's product assortment, even to the point of ignoring more profitable items that take more work to sell. We will be better off if we measure performance on things that are relevant to the company's overall goals.

Too High? Too Low? What Standard?

I've talked about measurement as a process. Now let's look at interpretation of the results. Every time you hear somebody saying that any item is "too low" or "too high," a little alarm should go off in your head. The implication is that some standard exists against which the offending item is being measured. The item that is considered to be too high or too low is either higher or lower than some expectation or lower or higher than that standard.

So your first question should be, What is the standard? The standard may be a budget or quota number. It may be last year's performance. It may be a competitor's results. Or it may be some vague variation of "I'll know a good number when I see it." In other words, to judge something as too high or too low as opposed to just plain higher or lower involves a value judgment that is based not on reality but on the perceptions and the agenda of the speaker.

Many so-called standards are founded only on opinion (usually the boss's opinion), and many so-called standards are, in fact, quite variable as time passes. Is 15% a good rate of profit? Only if the CEO thinks it is, and only as long as he or she thinks it is. This standard is not an Eternal Truth. The CEO might have thought that 15% was quite satisfactory, right up to yesterday's meeting of the board of directors, when the CEO was informed otherwise by consensus of the board. Now, the newly modified Eternal Truth is 18%, or whatever the CEO was told.

Here's an example of how variable standards are made to work by managers with short memories or flexible ethics. Did you greatly exceed your quota in part because one of your competitors made a serious strategic error? Then it's obvious that the successful result wasn't all due to your efforts, and that therefore your quota was set too low. Your performance bonus is now too high and must be adjusted (downward). Of course, that same manager will go to great lengths to prove that at his or her (more "strategic") level, the competitor's mistake should not be a factor in determining your manager's bonus.

Did you fail to make your quota because your competitor brought to market the improved product that you couldn't get approval for? Well, you didn't do so well. No, we can't always be adjusting quotas because of external conditions, or we'd have chaos. You win some and you lose some. (Sometimes, even when you win, you lose.) And by the way, your whining about this indicates that you may not be the team player we're looking for in our "family."

If the first question is, What is the standard? the second question, and one that you have to ask at the beginning of any project or task is, How will we know success when we see it? Can we agree, up front, that to constitute success, there is a tangible number of sales or sales dollars or profit dollars or percentage points or new inquiries or votes in a legislature?

Many managers claim to be in pursuit of something called maximum profit. A worthwhile concept, but if you stop and think about it, it will never be more than an abstract idea. It's something like the perfect lover: Could there not always be something more than that which is offered by the present situation?

In an atmosphere in which the thing we call reality is in fact subjective, we will have great difficulty getting anyone to commit to a hard-and-fast value that constitutes success, at least in writing for all to see. That's because, once a success point is revealed, it can't easily be changed or "adjusted to meet the evolving conditions of the marketplace which render our earlier projections inoperative." In other words, you met the goals we set, but it wasn't enough.

Here's another question: Are inventory costs too high? Well, how high is too high? What costs are actually charged to inventory? How much of the inventory is junk that nobody has yet had the guts to write off because (a) it would be an expense that would look bad and (b) it would lower the inventory's asset value on the books?

The list goes on. The financial process is driven by often conflicting personal considerations and perceptions within the company, not by reality. Inertia plays a part, too. There is a reluctance to change what works, even if it hasn't really been working for a while. Most important, everyone wants to have good numbers, because that's the way we keep score.

If you have the idea that people and personalities play a much more important role than you might have thought in setting, interpreting, and changing what looked like objective and real standards, welcome to the world. These are tools that will be used to make the folks who understand and control them look good.

So, you're making a presentation on a new project or product over which you have sweated blood. How will it be judged? By what standards? Find out as much as you can first, and remember that what you think is important may not be. As you make your presentation to CEOs or their designates, remember that in any presentation, the basic question each of your listeners is waiting for you to answer for them is, How will this help ME? The rest is details.

Five

An Economics Excursion

Economics, Science, Markets, and Demand

Those of you who have not had the good fortune to major in economics in college have missed some very valuable lessons that are buried in often excruciating detail. The irreverent view of economics is that it is the only subject in which the final exam questions each year are the same, but each year the correct answers to the questions are different.

The uncertainties underlying that assertion, which often leave economists with omelets on their faces after making predictions, is that economics is an attempt to apply scientific and mathematical principles to understanding and predicting an aspect of human behavior.

You should also be aware that before World War II, the academic subject that we know today as economics was taught under the title political economy. That's understandable, because politics is also dedicated to understanding and predicting an aspect of human behavior.

What is not so obvious is the link between economics and marketing, because the subjects are usually taught by different professors, each of whom has suspicions about the other. Yet, it is a link that you should know about, because it has an impact on your marketing efforts.

Utility Is Not Just Gas

When economists speak of *utility*, they are speaking of a thing's power to satisfy. It may seem to be a cumbersome term to most of us, but each profession has its words of art.

The economists theorize that people act in such a way as to maximize their utility; that is, they use their limited resources in a rational, prioritized way to make the economic buying decisions that make them the most satisfied.

Four different types of utility are involved here:

1. Form utility, which is provided when someone produces a product

2. Possession utility, that is, having the right to use or consume the product

3. Time utility, or the product being available when the consumer wants it

4. Place utility, which relates to a consumer's ability to gain access to a product

Now, the important thing here is that the economists recognize these influences on buying behavior and that satisfaction can come in part from more than just the product itself (form utility). As we are about to see, utility varies from person to person, and it varies over time as well.

The Economists' Curves

If, as marketers, we're going to study markets, the economists' concepts of supply and demand are helpful to us.

A *demand curve* is the graphic representation of the relationship between price and willingness to buy. It looks like Figure 5.1.

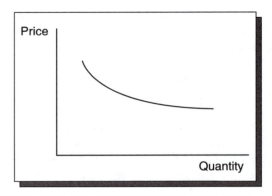

Figure 5.1   Demand Curve

The demand curve shown in Figure 5.1 simply means that people will buy more of something or less of something, depending on the price. With price on the vertical axis and quantity on the horizontal axis, the chart shows that the higher the price, the lower the quantity that will be demanded by the marketplace. The lower the price, the more that will be purchased by the marketplace. That seems obvious; we tend to buy more of something, or tend to be more likely to buy, when the price is lower than when it is higher. It's called the *law of diminishing demand*. There's a psychological corollary to this: The more we have of something, the less valuable any more of it is to us. The extreme case of this is demonstrated by an old Irving Berlin song title: "After You Get What You Want, You Don't Want It."

The economists aren't talking about individuals, they're talking about the "market," a group of buyers. But, as marketers continually point out to economists, the group is made up of individuals. The relationship holds true for most markets and for most products, although there are exceptions, mostly relating to goods driven by snob appeal ("Dahling, if it's not more expensive, I don't want it").

Note in Figure 5.1 that the exact shape of the demand curve, or numerical hash marks on the axes, are irrelevant to the conceptual discussion. The slope of the curve, however, is relevant to our discussion here.

The economists are there ahead of us when they speak of *inelastic demand* and *elastic demand*. It sounds scientific and complicated, but it isn't. To help you understand what's going on, let's look at different elasticities of demand.

Look at the two demand curves in Figure 5.2.

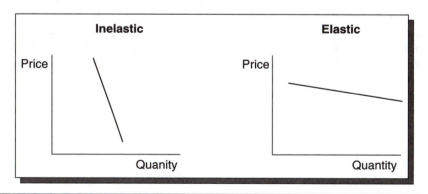

Figure 5.2   Inelastic and Elastic Demand Curves

For some commodities, a small change in the price can trigger a large swing in the demand. That's an *elastic* demand curve (the one on the right, or by the door). An elastic demand curve can quite likely result in a lower total revenue after a price hike, because many more people don't buy.

For other products and markets, the quantity demanded does not change much even with a large price change. That's an *inelastic* demand curve (the one on the left, or window side). That means that a price increase results in an increase in revenue, because fewer people would walk away. The point is that a product with an inelastic demand curve is much more profitable than a product with an elastic demand curve.

Now, what is the key to whether a product, *your* product, has a relatively unprofitable elastic demand curve or a relatively profitable inelastic demand curve? Can it be changed? Can we change it? Can we do things that make a demand curve more elastic? Well, of course we can; we're in Marketing.

That factor in determining elasticity of demand is *substitutability*, or whether there are or are not close substitutes available. If the customers have many alternatives, or a few real close ones, there is an elastic demand curve. If there are no close substitutes, the demand curve is inelastic. Put another way, elasticity is a question of how easy it is for the customer to do something else and tell you to go to hell.

So far, so good. Clearly, from the producer's standpoint, an inelastic demand curve is preferable to an elastic demand curve. But it's not all so scientific. In fact, if you remember that there is no such thing as objective reality, you're on the right track. This is because substitutability is something that is entirely within the mind of the customer. Each customer has his or her own idea of what could be an acceptable substitute and what is an acceptable substitute.

We know that customers approach the idea of substitutability with differing levels of intensity. What is an acceptable substitute for one person may not be an acceptable substitute for another person. Marriages have been known to break up over whether Brand Y is an acceptable substitute for Brand X. Here is a partial transcript of a marriage about to founder on the shoals of consumerism:

"This isn't Brand X."

"What's the big deal?"

"They are not the same!"

"Yes, they are."

"No, they're not!"

"Yes, they are."

"Well, this is not what I want!"

"Don't be a baby."

The only thing that matters to a customer (or, for that matter, to a significant other) is the perception of substitutability in the target customer's mind.

How can we change that? How can we make the demand curve for our product as inelastic as possible? We can do that by devoting our marketing effort to increasing the perception of our target customer groups that there is nothing else nearly as satisfying for their needs as the unique product we offer. We see this all the time in advertising: "There is only one Whizzo." "None Genuine Without This Label." "Accept No Substitutes."

Remember, this has nothing to do with reality. We see this attribution of uniqueness made every day, to gasoline, to milk, to bread, to cola drinks. These are products that have very little physical or chemical difference between them, yet we perceive them as more different than they really are and have favorites among them perhaps disproportionate to the actual difference.

Marketing and Elasticity

This book is not intended to be a treatise on market development, but the economists' way of measuring demand does illuminate the path toward pricing, which will be covered in the next chapter.

For now, let me state that everything we do as marketers is, or should be, designed to make the demand curve for our product less elastic and more inelastic. If you believe that your product doesn't lend itself to such individualization, you need only consider the Intel computer microprocessors. The Intel Corporation launched a promotion program called Intel Inside, with labels on personal computers and an advertising campaign to show that the features of their product were far superior (in their opinion) to the chips produced by other microprocessor manufacturers. At the risk of angering a phalanx of engineers, let us say that for the uses to which they will be put by most people, the microprocessors from the various manufacturers are functionally equivalent; there's no real difference. But the marketplace was convinced otherwise. Intel has positioned itself sufficiently above the masses to both generate a larger market share and to justify a higher price. They did this on a product that could have become a hidden generic component.

That's what understanding economics, demand curves, and substitutability can do for you—if you also remember that the "laws" of economics are based on people and their reactions, not on unchanging physical or mathematical principles.

Six

Pricing and Profitability

Pricing: Theory and Practice

So, how much will you charge for your product? We're covering that subject here because it is so closely related to profitability and to the real power of the customer-oriented marketing concept.

We can start with the economic concept of substitutability that we just covered. The key to pricing (and, for that matter, a significant key to understanding marketing) is figuring out what makes a demand curve elastic or inelastic for your product and your target market; that perceived substitutability affects the price.

But there is much mumbo jumbo on pricing. The most pervasive pricing problem faced by every marketing manager in every organization is this: You will get more help than you need, from everyone around you. Everyone has a theory, a formula, or a feeling, a gut instinct, or divine inspiration about what the prices should be. In fact, pricing is the single element in the marketing mix that everyone, in every discipline, feels themselves qualified to address.

Most of these businesspeople still suffer from the mistaken belief that they, rather than their customers, control their pricing. This results in some interesting instances of misplaced focus, with consequent adverse consequences for the business.

In some organizations, pricing is considered to be "too important to leave to the marketing people." Those are the companies that are fun to compete against, because they are usually behind the curve in terms of responsiveness. As one colleague put it, "In today's market, they are out of business; they just don't know it yet."

A True-False Quiz on Pricing

1. The price should be based on our actual total costs of producing the product.

2. Because customers consider price above all else, it is vital to have as low a price as our competitors will permit.

3. A lower price means greater sales volume and therefore a growing company with a better financial picture.

4. The best strategy if we are not the market leader is at least to match and preferably to undercut the leader's price.

5. Our largest and best customers are the ones we have to work hardest to keep, even if it means shaving our prices.

Yep, I did it to you again—the propositions above are all false. You knew that, of course. But you also know people in your organization who would get some of those questions wrong. Obviously, there is insufficient understanding of what a "price" really is.

What a "Price" Really Is

In line with our normal procedure, let's first look at a price from the customer's point of view. To the customer, the price is "whatever I have to give up to have this particular satisfaction of my need." This implies trade-offs in the expenditure of limited resources. Money spent to satisfy Need A will not be available for Needs B and C. The actual price of A or B or C makes up only one factor in the customer's overall consideration of alternatives to satisfying the need.

The concept used to describe this is *value*, defined as "the worth or desirability of a thing." The economists call it utility, or the power to satisfy. What we must remember is that worth or utility is in the customer's mind, not the producer's, and that each customer has a different set of needs and priorities.

The customer will buy if the price is lower than the utility or value the buyer believes to be present. It does not have to be much lower; just lower, or "worth it."

Value has nothing to do with reality. It has to do with the customer's perception of our offering, as opposed to other available offerings the customer knows about, that satisfy his or her need. Value is not only determined by the customer, it is also defined by the customer. Our entire marketing mix is designed to help that defining and determining process.

Remember, too, that the customer usually has the additional alternative of doing nothing: leaving the need unsatisfied for some defined or undefined time period or until a price is found that meets that customer's internally determined equilibrium point.

There's More Than Price Involved in Price

Remember, too, that the customer does not respond only to the product, or the price, but to the entire marketing mix of Product, Price, Place, and Promotion. Our product may have a higher perceived value if we can get it there faster or with certain bells and whistles or with installation or in the color we really want. It may have a higher perceived value because we have hammered home our message of highest quality, most reliable, and so on. It may have a higher value because we extend credit rather than requiring cash up front. We may have a better warranty/repair policy. All of the elements in the marketing mix play a role in the customer's decision; all of them contribute to value.

So, when prospects tell us that our price is "too high," what are they really saying? They're not just saying, "That's too many dollars." More accurately, they're saying, "There is not enough value here to justify my parting with that many dollars. I will select an alternate means of satisfying my need or I'll live with the need a while longer."

Does that sound obvious to you? Good. Because if you realize that the problem is insufficient value to justify the price in the customer's mind, rather than the absolute number of dollars involved, you are more likely to arrive at an optimum price.

It has become common to ask, Why does Company X charge so much? The fashionable answer is, "Because they can." This is often seen as a negative, couched in terms of nefarious plots, gouging, or monopolistic power. In most cases, it is no such thing. It is merely a normal situation in which a large enough group of target customers is satisfied with the value received and pays the price. Other people, who do not believe the value to be sufficient, may view the price with surprise, alarm, disdain, or outrage. But it's likely they weren't target customers anyway. A Rolls Royce is "too expensive"? Fine. Don't buy one.

The point is that price levels are a matter of opinion, not moral certainty, a matter of perception, not reality. If too few people acknowledge the value and pay the price, the price, and the company's fortunes, will descend. Indeed, the price would likely never have reached that high a level had greed not overruled marketing savvy.

People will indeed pay a higher price if they believe the value is there. Let me repeat that: People will indeed pay a higher price if they believe the value is there. And they will do so without complaint. If that were not so, there would be no luxury cars, no expensive stadium seats, no goods or services above the minimum price.

The concept of value and satisfaction versus minimum price extends even more to service industries. Customers will pay more for a service that they judge to be worth more. Why do some lawyers bill at (and get) $300 per hour and more, whereas others receive $100 per hour? Obviously, the $300 lawyer is perceived as worth more. I am reminded of a public agency I worked with years ago that actually did hire the law firm that had submitted the bid with the lowest hourly rates. The legal tangles that ensued showed that they got the quality of work they paid for.

A Small Digression on Quality

Quality. If there is one word that has become a watchword, a byword, a buzzword, it is *quality*. We have Quality Circles, Quality Seminars, Quality Programs. We have TQM, QRP, BQS, and the international "standard," ISO 9000 (which, unfortunately, is often treated as a paper exercise that generates volumes of justifying documentation more often than real answers and improvements). Quality can be Total, Thorough, Premium, Advanced, Job One, Our Motto, Pretty Good, Our Mission, and Our Albatross.

From a marketing standpoint, what is quality? It is sufficient value, reliability, and so on to satisfy the customer. Quality is not an internal touchstone; it must begin with the customer's requirements, needs, and, yes, prejudices—not the preferences of our company's chief engineer or CEO. ("Vot? Zey don't like Wagner?") Quality does not exist by itself, or as an end in itself. Do not let the "religious revivalist" approach to internal quality improvements distract you from the reality that quality derives from the customer's needs, perceptions, requirements, and specifications.

Price Versus Cost

The most startling result of our discussion of substitutability, elasticity, and the customer's perception of value is the realization that our design and production costs really do not enter into the process at all. Now, the "pricing helpers" from the Engineering or Accounting Departments are likely to tell us about the Iron Law that prices are determined based on our costs. So, many companies still set their prices as a multiple of their costs. They have developed and refined complex internal formulas whereby the direct costs are massaged, perhaps doubled, multiplied by a fraction of the overhead costs, divided by the square root of the CEO's social security number, and then rounded upward to the nearest 95 cents.

Why?

Although we want to cover our costs and earn a profit, our costs are not relevant to the customer's decision-making process. Customers do not care about our costs; they care about their needs.

By the way, one of the stupidest things many companies do is announce a price increase "made necessary because our costs are going up." Who the hell cares about your costs? Do you think the customer will say, soothingly, "That's all right, you poor thing; we understand; it's OK"??

Most self-respecting customers will be turned off by a seller's whining about rising costs. (Aren't you?) Think of the nonprofit agencies (for example, public television stations) whose appeals for funds are studded with whimperings about increased costs, insufficiency of resources To Meet the Growing Needs Out There, and so on. Frankly, the donors could not care less; they are motivated to contribute by their perceptions of the agency's success in doing its job, not by the difficulties involved.

Why do we use cost-based pricing? Because it's easy. If we set prices based on our costs, we use known numbers. It is internal and therefore more controllable, more comfortable. It also produces prices that are, almost by definition, either too high or too low. A price that is too high results in reduced sales. A price that is too low yields a lower margin. Either way, profit is hampered.

Markups and Breakeven

A *markup* is an amount added to the cost of an item to determine its selling price. In most retailing operations, the markup is calculated using a percentage of the selling price. So, if dealers buy an item at wholesale for $6 and sell it for $10, they are said to be operating with a 40% markup. After all, $4 is 40% of $10. And $4 is also 66.6% of $6, but we use the selling price as the base.

Figure 6.1 shows the situation where sellers add a 33.3% markup to their cost. That's 33.3% of the selling price. Note that 33.3% of the selling price is also 50% of the cost (which is 66.6% of the selling price).

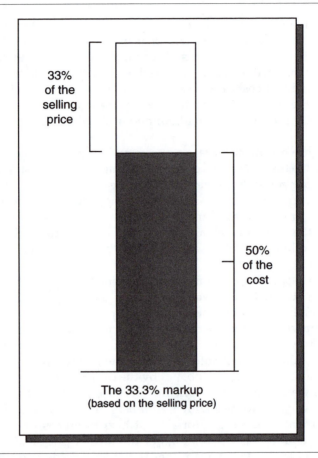

33%
of the
selling
price

50%
of the
cost

The 33.3% markup
(based on the selling price)

Figure 6.1   Markup

It gets worse. In many industries, the price all along the channel of distribution is calculated based on the selling price. The manufacturer may sell to the distributor for "50 off," or 50% of the selling price. The distributor sells to the dealer for "40 off," which is where we came in. But in some industries, the cost is used as the basis for the calculation, as in "cost plus 20%." The main point is that you have to know which base figure is being used by the people with whom you're dealing.

But businesses can get into trouble if they consider only the markup and assume that they're doing well. "After all, I'm making 40% on everything I sell; why am I not doing better?" The reason is that if you're not selling enough goods and services at that markup, you're not covering all of your costs. Quite a few retailers have power-driven themselves straight into bankruptcy by not understanding this.

This is where we should take a first look at the concept of breakeven, in which we consider how many units we will have to sell in order to cover our costs. We'll go into it in detail later, but for now, look at the simplified diagram in Figure 6.2.

The Total Revenue and Total Cost lines both increase as we sell more units. The Total Revenue curve starts at zero. If we sell nothing, we receive nothing. And we receive the revenue amount per unit for each unit we sell.

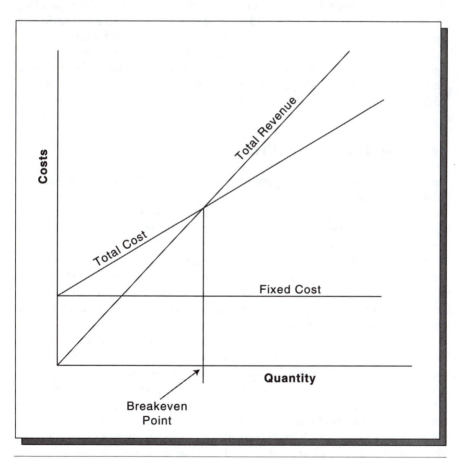

Figure 6.2   Breakeven Point

But our Total Cost curve does not start at zero, because even if we sell no units, we do have costs associated with operating the business. So, until we sell enough units to cover all the costs, we'll lose money. At some point, if we have priced our products properly, we sell enough units to cover all the costs; that's called the *breakeven point*. Each unit we sell after that contributes to our profit. But there is no profit until we reach the breakeven point.

Many firms use average-cost pricing, which means adding some reasonable markup to the average cost of a product. The average cost per unit is determined by dividing the total cost for the last year by the number of units produced.

It's easy to do, but average-cost pricing can be a formula for losing money. The basic problem is that this approach doesn't consider the effect on total cost caused by different levels of output. As with any markup, if you sell too few units to cover all of your costs, you lose money.

And there are different types of costs that you must consider when setting a price: variable costs and fixed costs. But that's for the next chapter. Right now, let's get back to pricing and our customers; remember, they don't care about our costs.

Sensitive Pricing for Profit

Remember how we defined profit in Chapter 1: the amount by which our customers believe our products to be worth more than the resources we expended on those products. Similarly, loss is the amount by which present and potential customers believe our products to be worth less than the resources we have expended.

The setting of prices, therefore, has a direct impact on profit. In fact, pricing can have more of an impact on profit than the level of sales achieved. The elastic demand curves we covered in the previous chapter have shown us that high sales can very easily be accompanied by low profits, or even by no profits at all.

The question of how readily some of our customers will abandon us if we raise the price, or will flock to us if we lower it, is called *price sensitivity*; it relates to the elasticity of those demand curves. The level of sensitivity has been said to vary depending on the product, the stage of the product's life cycle, the state of the economy, and so on. But a more important factor, and one that is usually overlooked, is the nature of the target customer group. It's not the product that determines sensitivity, it's the people who are, or are not, sensitive. That sensitivity is more likely to vary by type of customer than by type of product. The question is not, Is the price too high? but Is the perceived value of our marketing mix sufficient to justify a higher price?

How can we determine price sensitivity? Well, we could conduct a survey, but the results aren't likely to be useful.

"Sir, would you continue to buy this if the price went up by 5%? By 10%? Sir? Sir??"

A better analysis would keep track of the prices of our product, and the available substitutes, over time. What happened when a competitor raised a price? What happened when we last raised our price? There are mathematical formulas that can help with price sensitivity analysis, but it really isn't a math problem.

There's another factor in the price sensitivity analysis, and that's the sensitivity range. This, too, is perceptual, but it's generally stated as the "acceptable" range of prices for such a product, beyond which sensitivity increases sharply. A personal computer with a given configuration may be a great buy at $1,399. You could charge $1,499 and lose some customers. But at some point, say $1,700, an extra degree of resistance sets in, where almost the whole world will say that regardless of brand name, warranty, delivery, hand-holding, and all the other value-adding features, this personal computer "just ain't worth that much." So, if you're already near the high end of the sensitivity range, you're in for a serious shock if you raise the price above that psychological upper limit.

Now, if you survey customers, you can get some honest answers about the sensitivity range. Your marketing research can also get input from your salespeople, distributors, and dealers. If you're doing this on a continuing basis, you probably have a good idea of that range and the changes in it over time.

Of course, the best way to raise a price is to do so concurrent with an improvement in some area of the marketing mix that raises the perceived value at the same time. Many companies test price sensitivity by making a limited test of a price change, with or without value enhancements. Different enhancements might also be tested against each other. This could be regionally, or "for a limited time only," or for one part of your product assortment or target market group.

The most intriguing question is, Is there something we can do to our marketing mix that would not just make an incremental change within the range but would create a whole new price sensitivity range, based on a marketing mix element that sufficiently differentiates our "new" product from customer perceptions of the old ones? Something that makes the perceived value of our product or variation "more valuable"? Isn't that what Toyota did, in figuring that people might be more willing to pay a great deal more for a car called a Lexus than for a car called a Toyota?

Isn't that what the beer microbreweries are seeking to do: to create a new product category called premium beers, with a price sensitivity range in which Miller and Bud are irrelevant?

Marginal Revenue

For you to gain a better insight into pricing and the kinds of things that trip up many managers and accountants, we'll stop here and consider the concept of *marginal revenue*. It relates to the demand curve we looked at in Chapter 5.

Marginal revenue, like marginal cost (which we'll cover in Chapter 7), is the revenue we can expect from the sale of the next product we add to our output. In other words, if we make 100 widgets, the marginal revenue is the amount we can expect to receive for the 101st widget. Furthermore, marginal revenue for the 102nd widget is going to be different from the marginal revenue for the 101st widget, marginal revenue for the 103rd will be different from the 102nd, and so on.

Note that marginal revenue is different from the average revenue per unit—it's often considerably different. The average revenue is easily determined: Divide the total revenue by the number of units. Marginal revenues are more difficult to estimate, because they involve a changing rate of change. That's where calculus can come in handy, but not right here.

When we're looking for information upon which to base decisions, however, marginal revenue becomes more relevant than average revenue. It's relevant because marginal revenue is generally lower than the average revenue.

That's because of the nature of the demand curves shown in Chapter 5. They slope downward to show that more goods will be sold at a lower price than at a higher price. We choose only one production level (based on an estimated sales level, I hope!) at a given point on the demand curve.

The implication is that as we make more widgets, we can expect to get less revenue per widget for each additional one we make. Figure 6.3 shows this graphically. The customers who will purchase those next additional widgets are customers who haven't bought already. These are likely to be customers who didn't feel the value was there at a higher price.

This condition trips up the financial people who use average revenue as the basis for their calculations, because the actual revenue almost always turns out to be less than what they predicted it would be. Beware of the assumption that there is an infinite market out there at current average price levels. Those who haven't bought yet are less likely to pay the higher prices paid by those who have bought already.

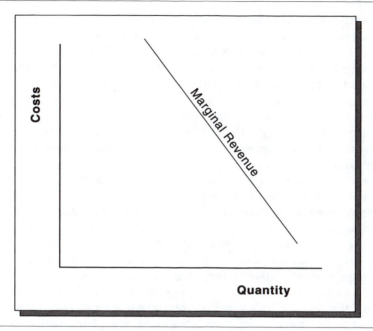

Figure 6.3   Marginal Revenue

But there's more than math involved in pricing. There are also considerations of objectives and priorities.

What Is the Company's Objective?

In setting prices for its product(s), what is your company's *objective*?

That's an obvious question, but the answers often are not so obvious. In fact, it's appalling how many companies really don't have an answer beyond "to make a profit, of course!" or "to beat our competition, dummy!"

Right. But for any marketing person, that kind of rah-rah spirit is quicksand, because the objectives are not definite. This may be true despite a recent set of meetings within the company to focus on "our mission and our goals." Any objective must be clearly stated in terms of definite target numbers and time frames. "We're going to increase profits" is meaningless. "We're shooting for a 10% profit by July 1" is definite.

Let's look at some alternate pricing objectives and strategies.

We could set prices based on *profit-related objectives*. In doing so, there are three general alternatives: maximum profit, target profit, and sufficient profit.

A *maximum profit* objective says, "We'll charge what the market will bear; there are no close substitutes, and people will buy our product because of its value." The drawback to this objective is that sales volume will likely be limited, and one or more competitors will be very highly motivated to enter the market that you have shown to be so profitable. "You're Never Alone." Also, "maximum" profit is a concept; trying to measure it usually dissolves into opinion and argument.

One pricing strategy consistent with a maximum profit objective is known as *skimming*, derived from setting high initial prices to skim the cream from the market at first and then lowering the price as the market becomes more saturated. Computer chip manufacturers do this with new, more powerful models. If one waits, the same device will be available at much lower prices later. Book publishers form another group that practices skimming, with the price highest at the time a new, highly publicized book hits the market. Those prices too will fall, as the more intent target groups become saturated (or satiated, depending on the book).

A *target profit* objective is very definite, which is why administrative types in a company push for it. It's easy to judge (the light's better here). You either made the 10% target or you didn't. It's also easy for top management to determine which products should be kept and which should be dropped. Just look at the numbers. Here's the cutoff point. Simple. And it's very difficult to criticize decisions made on such a bedrock policy.

The danger with target pricing is precisely that binary approach, in which asking for consideration of underlying causes is often interpreted by others as telling a story or justifying your less-than-effective existence.

The *sufficient profit* objective is a variation of the target return approach; we just want to make enough to cover our needs, to satisfy our stockholders, and so on. Companies back in to such an objective when they tie pricing directly to their costs. Nonprofit organizations generally have as their objective the coverage of their operating costs. That's a zero target.

But profit is only one type of objective that we might pursue in setting prices. Many companies, although not ignoring profit, concentrate on *sales-related objectives*. Those could be expressed in terms of sales volume, dollar sales, or share of the market. Let's stop for a moment. Has it become clear to everybody that a pricing strategy designed to achieve one objective will not achieve others? Is it clear that some of the various objectives conflict with each other? OK. Just checking.

A *sales volume* objective involves a lessened importance on dollar sales. "We will be selling 10,000 units per month by next October." The large unanswered question is, At what price will customers buy 10,000 units a month by next October? And will we have made a profit if they do?

A *dollar sales* objective says, "We will be selling $300,000 worth of products per month by next October." Unit volume is less important here, and the focus is on revenue. Fewer units at a higher price can generate as much revenue as more units at a lower price.

A *market share* objective involves a longer-range strategy. That's because the market leader is in a very powerful position in the market. The market leader, the firm with the largest percentage share of total sales, is also almost always the most profitable firm in the market in the long run. That's partially because of economies of scale (which we will cover in Chapter 7 on costs).

Penetration pricing policies come into play in the quest for market share. These are the diametric opposite of skimming strategies. Penetration pricing sets a low price to capture as large a share of the market as possible. Never mind costs; the objective here is to set a price so low that it causes our present and potential competitors to consider investing their resources in other areas and not competing with us.

Penetration pricing is not necessarily the same thing as setting introductory low prices. The introductory strategy assumes that the price will be raised later if market conditions (success) justify the increase. Penetration pricing for market share does not necessarily imply price increases, although later improved versions of a product that add value may be priced higher.

There are still other objectives that may govern pricing policy. One in particular is common particularly in calm or stagnant markets. Essentially, it's the "don't make waves" objective. Companies compete on nonprice grounds, but not on price. They all charge essentially the same price. The classic example of this is the road intersection with four gas stations, each a different brand but all with the same prices. Competition comes from brand recognition, credit cards, which side of the street, signage, and so on. That works until somebody decides to make a wave.

Pricing Policies You Should Have

On the assumption that you would rather try to manage your pricing than have it manage you, there are some policies and strategies that you should consider. Many people are surprised to find that they have a choice at all in some areas, but they do. Here are some of the questions.

Will You Price at the Front End or the Back End?

You can set the price(s) at which your distributors and dealers buy and let them control the prices of sales down the channel to the ultimate consumers. Or you can set a list price or suggested retail price for the final consumer and work the dealer discounts back from that. Be careful here; if the list price becomes too much of a fiction, you could be in legal trouble.

How Flexible Are Your Prices?

Will everyone be charged the same price, all the time? Or will different prices be charged under different conditions? Discounts that provide different prices to different customers are not uncommon, under certain circumstances. Discounts usually relate to quantities purchased or seasonality or payment terms. Allowances usually relate to something done in exchange for a lower price. Although some customers may complain, discounts based on cost differentials are not uncommon nor are allowance arrangements.

The reason it helps to set all of this out in advance is simple: If you let your people play it by ear, revenues will effectively go down as people make deals with good customers or someone makes a costly mistake.

How Will Prices Vary Over Time?

Both the skimming and penetration policies also touch on another aspect of pricing strategy: that the strategy will vary over the product's life cycle. As I said, better to plan for it than to have it happen all over you. As a product ages, it becomes a candidate for price cuts. Alternately, cost increases may make it desirable to increase a price. What's your plan for possible improvements in the marketing mix to accompany price rises to make them more palatable?

How Much Is That in Dollars?

If you're selling in other countries, you're dealing in another country's currency. That means keeping track of currency exchange rates. Fluctuation of exchange rates and the high rates of inflation in some countries will have to be taken into consideration. Note that this isn't always bad. Mercedes-Benz automobiles were noted for holding their value (i.e., not depreciating very much) during the 1980s. What many people didn't notice was that much of that value came about because the German mark was becoming stronger against the dollar. Psychology did the rest.

In addition to currency fluctuations, other costs will appear that are unique to each country. For example, what additional packaging and labeling requirements are there? Must the product be modified in some way to comply with a given nation's laws or customs? What is the cost of such modifications? Is credit going to be a problem? What tariffs are applicable?

There are also differences in consumer groups' perceptions of value, not only between countries but between different regions of any country. Your additional costs may push the price of your marketing mix above that which is considered a reasonable value in that country. All of this enters into the creation of pricing strategy.

When you hear someone talking about a global product strategy or a worldwide price, you should immediately become suspicious. The cultural differences around the world are sufficiently great, and sufficiently unpredictable, as to trap those who believe they can rise above the regional or national idiosyncrasies of their customers.

Pricing of Services

Where services are concerned, their intangible nature makes the customer's perception of value even more important. Why is Lawyer A able to bill at $300 per hour while Lawyer B bills at only $100 per hour? The answer is that a sufficient number of present and potential customers believe that Lawyer A's services are worth it. Not only is Lawyer A good, but people know it.

But how to price a service? The standard approach is to take the service provider's compensation and apply a multiplier to it, arriving at a billing rate per hour. For some standardized tasks, a flat fee can be established, based on time and the hourly rate.

An approach likely to yield a higher profit is to base the price on the value of the service to the customer, which is, of course, the same basis that the customer is using for the decision to purchase. If a 100-hour consulting task can save a client $100,000 or raise revenue by $100,000, the saving is $1,000 per hour of effort. How much of that is the customer willing to spend to achieve that saving? Half? One quarter? Negotiation will ensue.

The danger in pricing services is that the scope of services to be provided must be set forth as definitely as possible, with stated deliverable items and limits on correction and editing iterations. If this is not done, the provider can put in many unexpected hours and the client may still feel unsatisfied.

For many professional services, a case can be made that marginal revenue increases for added hours, which is precisely the reverse of the conventional wisdom for tangible products. The reason is that if professionals are successful, more people will want their services. Professionals will shortly be very busy. A new client may be taken on, but only at a billing rate higher than clients acquired in leaner times. The result is a higher marginal revenue.

Now, when increasing demand approaches finite capacity, the strategy is to raise the price. This means that some present clients may elect to go elsewhere. But the ones who stay will be paying a higher average rate. As long as the perceived value is there, the price is not too high.

One more consideration: Reread this section on services again, this time considering your service and its perceived value to an employer or customer. Are you being paid in line with the value you provide?

Seven

Costs and Profitability

Costs, Real and Imagined

It may sound silly that to succeed as a marketer you must understand costs. But, you might think, isn't that for the Production and Finance people? Multiply the cost per widget by the number of widgets involved and you arrive at a total cost. Marketing people focus on customers and prices, not costs.

Marketing people also have to understand costs, and, more important, they have to understand how people think about costs. This is especially important, because not everything that people think about costs is true. For example, we just talked about widgets, cost per widget, and total cost. But the calculation that is done more often is the reverse of what I described above: We start with a number of cost components, add them up to get a total cost, and then divide by the number of widgets produced to get the average cost per widget. If we increase production by 50%, will we still have the same cost per widget? The temptation is to take our average cost and multiply that by the new production quota, at which point we enter unreality. It doesn't work that way.

I have already discussed the retailer who can't understand why, even with a high markup, there isn't enough money at the end of the month. A similar problem is faced by manufacturers, providers of services, and, in fact, anybody who runs a business. I'll take up the subject of breaking even in the next chapter. For now, let's look at our costs.

Variable, Fixed, and Somewhere in Between

First of all, a cost is the expenditure of resources to achieve a desired end. Essentially, we have to consider three kinds of costs, depending on how they vary as production levels change. They are variable costs, fixed costs, and semivariable costs.

Variable costs are directly affected by the number of units produced. If no units are produced, the cost is zero. For each unit produced, there is a materials component and a labor component. For example, we may calculate that each unit involves $3 worth of material and $20 worth of labor to produce. That's a variable cost of $23 per unit. Ten units would have a total variable cost of $230, 20 units $460, and so on.

Fixed costs do not go up or down as we produce more or fewer units. Examples are the CEO's base salary, the rent or mortgage on the factory, and the costs of the front office. Those costs would be there even if no units are produced, as long as the business is open.

In between fixed and variable costs are *semivariable costs*. These costs go up in large steps with different production quantities. The best example is a factory that installs a second (or third, or fourth) machine to handle increased production. Up to 100 units, one machine can handle the job. But for the next 100 units, a second machine will be required, and a third for the 100 units after that, and so on. The costs are not fixed, but there is a definite jump in cost between the 100th unit and the 101st unit produced because of the semivariable cost of the new machine.

The total cost is therefore the sum of all of the three types of costs applicable to the units produced. Figure 7.1 is like Figure 6.2, but it is a bit more detailed. It shows a graphic representation of the total cost and its components and how the costs vary with rates of production.

Although they are helpful as training aids, the mischief in Figure 7.1 is that it shows a straight line for variable costs. But the actual variable costs are not linear. The fact is that the units between 290 and 300 may be more expensive per unit than the units between 220 and 230, because the production at the high end of that range may involve a stretch because of more overtime or premium prices paid for materials to get delivery. Alternatively, a higher quantity may show a lower unit cost because of a learning curve in labor and a lower per-unit material cost at higher quantities.

All of this means that you have to work to understand and make estimates about your actual situation, rather than relying on mindless financial rules of thumb. Regardless of how much it looks like the real, exact, unchangeable thing, this estimating process is not an exact science.

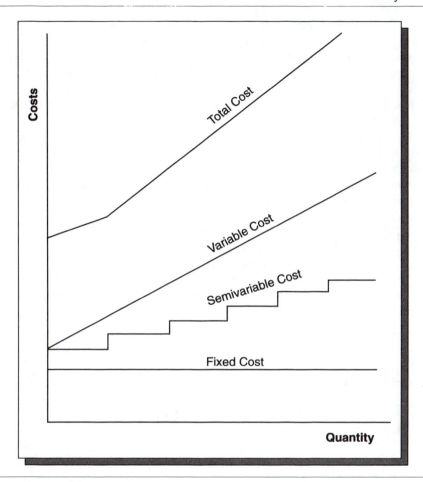

Figure 7.1   Cost Curves

Cost Allocation

The image is part of our folklore: It shows five or six diners in a restaurant who have just been presented with a single check for the entire meal. They are trying to figure out how much each of them should pay toward the total amount, including tax and tip. The ensuing scramble has been known to ruin what up to that time had been an enjoyable meal. Unless, of course, one member of the party is an accountant, in which case that individual cheerfully volunteers to figure, to the penny, how much each party owes. Most of the time, however, everybody "approximates" until there is enough money in the pile to cover the check and the tip. Some diners pay more than their share, some pay less.

If more than one party shares the use of a resource, the question of cost allocation, or determining how much of the total cost each party should pay, inevitably arises. In most cases, it's not even as obvious a division as the restaurant example; cost allocation is not an exact or straightforward process.

Here's an example of how something that looks simple and obvious at first turns out to be a nonscientific problem. Figure 7.2 is the simplified plan view of a building whose floor space is shared equally by two departments, A and B. The electricity supply to the building comes through one common meter, and each month's power company bill shows only the total for the building.

How is the cost of power allocated between the two departments? Yes, I know, the ideal solution is two separate meters, but until we can get approval for that capital expenditure, how do we divide the cost?

The obvious answer is to split the power bill according to the square footage, or the percentage of the building occupied by each department.

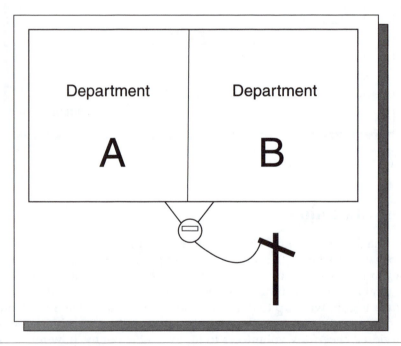

Figure 7.2   Building Plan With Shared Power Costs

Costs and Profitability 69

That's 50–50 in this case. This solution also has the benefit of being very little work for the accountants, which is quite often the reason why the accountants choose such a cost division. No need to make more work than is necessary; just divide the bill by 2 and allocate half of the cost to each department. That's what happened in our company; the allocation decision was made back in 1974.

But is it accurate? If, for example, Department A is a standard office but Department B is refining aluminum, there's a clear difference in power consumption. The time factor is also relevant. A cost allocation decision made in 1974 is quite likely to have been made under different conditions; yet in too many organizations, the effects persist long after the conditions change, because nobody brings it up.

So, if a request now comes forward for a full analysis of power consumption, with the purpose of achieving a more accurate and fair division of the power costs, what is the one thing we know for sure?

We know for sure that the request came from Department A.

Dividing the bill in half favors Department B, because part of its electricity is being paid for by Department A. That can be vitally important to Department A's manager, because his or her departmental profit picture is being negatively affected by having to shoulder part of Department B's costs in addition to Department A's costs. Lower profit, lower performance rating, lower bonus, many consequences follow.

We also know that no one in Department B would make such a request for a usage study, because Department B has nothing to gain from such an analysis. (Notice that the concept of objective fairness rarely if ever enters the picture in these situations.)

Well, now that the question has been raised, just what is the best way to allocate the power costs? It is not likely that Department B will allow this assault on its cozy cost structure to go unanswered. Alternate approaches to divide the power bill will surface for consideration, among them:

- Division based on the number of employees in each department
- Division based on the portion of the company's revenue generated by the two departments
- Division based on the portion of the company's profit generated by the two departments (which most likely is not the same as a division based on revenue)
- Division based on the relative asset value of each department's facilities
- Division based on the size of each department's total expenses, on the theory that the larger, "wealthier" department should bear a larger share of the costs (this approach, by the way, can be recognized as a foundation of U.S. tax policy)

Now, let's stop and look at what has really happened here. Department A has raised the issue of an "unfair" allocation of costs, which helps Department B at the expense of Department A. Department B would never raise the issue. Neither would Headquarters Accounting, which likes to keep things simple. Once raised, the process becomes one of getting a decision from higher authority to change or not to change the allocation.

Let's play Omnipotent Being for a moment and state the reality that Department B is in fact using 70% of the electricity that goes into that building and Department A is using 30% of the power. (The departments don't know that exact number, but we do.) Yet, the cost allocation has Departments A and B sharing the cost equally.

So what happens? Both sides present their cases to the decision-making authority higher up in the company. On the basis of the presentations and on a desire to reach some kind of vague consensus or compromise, the decision maker realizes that Department B should pay at least something more, and decrees that the allocation henceforth shall be 60% to Department B and 40% to Department A. Thus it is written; thus it shall be done.

But is it right? Well, it's certainly not accurate, and it's certainly not scientific. But 60–40 is now the approved cost allocation ratio. Department A gets something, Department B loses something, and life goes on.

Or, in an alternate scenario, Department B agrees to a realignment of executive spaces in the parking lot that favors Department A, and Department A agrees to settle for less than the 70% it knows it should have. Now, that's even less scientific, or objective, but it happens. It's in Department B's best interest to settle for 60–40, because a real analysis would hurt them more.

What have we learned?

1. How costs are allocated can have a definite impact on a department's profitability.

2. Most cost allocations do not accurately reflect a true picture, especially if they were made more than a couple of years ago.

3. The manager who ignores this situation is far more likely to be in the position of Department A's manager than Department B's manager; that is, he or she is paying part of somebody else's costs and shows a lower profit as a result.

4. Cost allocation is in fact a process more often resolved by negotiation than by Eternal Truths.

5. Ultimately, the "right" cost allocation is the one that is approved by the higher-level decision maker.

Do not assume that all is well where you are. Consider the case of one student who came to class after attending the one in which we covered this material. His report:

After the class, I checked some of the costs on our Income Statement, and I found that our department was being charged for the cost of every cell phone and pager in the company. Turned out that it was because our department was the first one to get cell phones, a number of years ago. The accountants saw a "Cell Phone" account and just charged everything to it ever since, even though the costs had nothing to do with our department.

Another:

An accountant came by with a $3,500 voucher for me [a marketing product manager] to sign, covering the costs of changing some production line tooling. I said, "No, those aren't Marketing costs."

The accountant said, "Don't worry about it, that's the way it's being done."

Turned out that no, those weren't really Marketing costs, but rather the costs of revising tooling to correct errors they made. My two predecessors had never questioned vouchers like these, and the other department was able to offload some of its costs. Then they got angry because I questioned it, but management decided I was right.

You will have to find your own balance between righteous defense of what is obviously correct and being a team player.

Why a Toilet Seat Costs $600

There can also be numbers that don't quite make sense, caused by the allocation of indirect costs to the units in a production run. It wasn't too long ago that there was a great Congressional uproar about $600 toilet seats installed in a Navy airplane. Many people were outraged by the idea that a toilet seat should cost that kind of money, when a pretty good one can be had for less than $20 at any home supply store. But the toilet seats really did cost that much, and it won't take us long to get to the, er, bottom of the matter. As I said, the answer lies in allocation of costs. Let's take a similar but fictional example.

Were these standard toilet seats? No. Standard toilet seats would be too heavy and would not have fitted into the cramped quarters on the chemical-type toilet to be put into the plane. The toilet seat had to be custom fabricated, and was designed to fit, er, flush with other paneling in the airplane.

Designed? Yes. And airplane designers don't come cheap. Neither do draftsmen, toolmakers, and managers. Particularly managers. Let's look at an example of how these things happen. These aren't the numbers for the real airplane in the story; I think those were classified. In any case, Figure 7.3 shows how a toilet seat can be shown to cost more than $600

Whizzo Airplane Works Toilet Seat Cost Analysis

	Hours	Cost/Hr ($)	Cost ($)
Engineering:			
Design–seat	12	50	600
Design–interface	12	50	600
Design review	4	80	320
Drafting	12	30	360
Specification writing	6	40	240
Specification approval	2	80	160
Approval package prep.	4	50	200
Review of package	2	80	160
Revisions	16	50	800
Review of revisions	28	0	160

Total Engineering Direct			3,600
Engineering overhead (40%)			2,128
Total Engineering			5,728
Manufacturing:			
Planning	3	50	150
Shop drawings-seat	3	40	120
Shop drawings-tooling	3	40	120
Shop drawings-assembly	3	40	120
Review	2	100	200
Form & tooling			
Labor	25	30	750
Materials			300
Purchasing cost	6	30	180
Shop scheduling	2	35	70
	Seats	Cost/seat	
Fiberglass	18	3	54
Labor	18	20	360

Total Manufacturing Direct			2,424
Manufacturing overhead (60%)			1,454
Total Manufacturing			3,878

Subtotal, all costs:			9,606
General & Admin. overhead (15%)			1,441

Grand Total Cost			11,047
Divide by seats	18		**613.72**

Figure 7.3   Toilet Seat Cost Analysis

each by the Whizzo Airplane Works cost analysis, and gives us a platform to explore various kinds of costs.

First of all, the contract was for 18 airplanes, of a special-purpose type. Standard components that would fit in the plane were not available; the lavatory facility was part of the overall design effort. The design work that was done, and all the review and approvals by the senior managers of the airplane factory and the Navy, carried engineering costs that were to be incurred whether one plane or a thousand were built.

The hours spent on the toilet seat design and the costs per hour (including wages and fringe benefits for the engineering personnel involved to calculate their billing rates) totaled $3,600. This also included the review and coordination process to make sure that the seat actually would fit in the overall design of the plane. Specifications and other technical documents also had to be drawn up to make sure the Navy did not get a substandard product. These were work hours that could reasonably be "charged to the job," or direct costs. They were taken directly from the time sheets of the employees involved.

The 40% engineering overhead burden, or $2,128, represents the estimated (read "guess") overhead costs of the engineering effort, and was based on a Defense Department audit of Whizzo's actual costs from the previous year. The overhead costs include all the Engineering Department's accounting, secretarial, office rent and utility costs, computer supplies, paper clips, and so on and the expenses of getting ready for the audit. The cost of the Defense Department auditors is not in this number; that's still more, which we taxpayers paid. The overhead cost percentage, often called a "burden" (one of the more appropriate terms used in accounting), was added to the direct costs. So the total engineering cost was $5,728.

Notice here that the more indirect costs a company can stuff into its overhead factors or burdens, the more money it will receive for each hour of work expended, because the overhead factor is a multiplier that is added to the direct cost. I'll cover that more thoroughly in a minute, but notice the practical effect. It means that the company's financial folks try to include as much of the company's total expenses as they can get away with, including the costs of executive lunch meetings, the company airplane, the party in Acapulco—excuse me, the directors' working meeting in Acapulco—you get the idea. That is why the government has auditors, who habitually disallow the inclusion of as many of these questionable costs as possible in the overhead calculation. A specific example in the case of engineering burdens is computer equipment: How much of it is actually used for engineering and how much for other purposes?

Now for the costs of manufacturing. The design called for a form-fitted, fiberglass seat and chemical toilet cover, hinged to allow easy removal of the chemical tank. That meant that not only did manufacturing drawings and production plans for the seat have to be prepared from the engineering blueprints, but also the design work for the forms and tooling had to be done. Once designed (and approved), the actual tooling and forms then had to be built. Only after all that do we get to the $3 per seat material cost and the $20 per seat labor cost of actually producing each seat. (What? You thought this thing would just be hacked out of wood by itinerant craftspeople?)

Yes, each seat actually "cost" only $23 each. But the total cost of producing the toilet seats for 18 airplanes was $11,047. When you divide $11,047 by 18, you flush out a per-seat cost of $613.72.

And that didn't include the salary and overhead of the federal inspectors and administrators involved in supervising the contractor.

Direct and Indirect Costs, or, Over Whose Head?

We have just seen an example of *cost allocation*. The total costs not directly involved with the manufacture of the toilet seats were allocated over the 18 seats to come up with the number that provided such entertainment for members of Congress (who either should have known better or who did know better and were being outraged for the sake of the cameras).

The material and labor costs, and other expenses, that are directly identified with, attributable to, and chargeable to the products (or services) themselves are called *direct* costs. Those costs that are involved in running the business regardless of production level are *indirect* costs, often called *overhead* costs.

Why are they called overhead costs? Most likely because they apply to keeping the roof over our heads at any level of production. Because of the complexity that can be involved in calculating indirect costs, one of my colleagues years ago may have been close to the truth when he said, "Overhead costs? They're darn sure over my head."

Indirect costs by their nature cannot be directly tied to a unit of output. They may not be tied directly to any given product line. Where they cannot be so identified, they are distributed among the product lines, units of output, departments, cost centers, and so on, *on some agreed-upon basis*. This brings us back to what we were saying in Chapter 1: Allocation of indirect costs is the product of law and negotiation, not revealed and unchangeable truth.

As we have seen, allocation is a mathematical calculation that attributes costs to units of input or output. Remember, just because a cost allocation can be done accurately does not mean that it makes sense. The

$600 toilet seat is a classic example of allocation taken beyond common sense. It's a triumph of technique over purpose.

Once we recognize these limitations, allocation of indirect costs can help us to understand the true costs of our activities.

Is Overhead a Burden?

I alluded earlier to the 40% Engineering burden, 60% Manufacturing burden, and 15% General and Administrative (G&A) burden at the Whizzo Airplane Works.

These burdens are calculated percentages of direct costs added to the direct costs in order to allocate indirect costs, including fringe benefits and support expenses. Those numbers are usually derived by taking last year's indirect costs (or a multiyear average) and measuring them against the direct costs involved. When, for example, we speak of a "15% G&A burden," it means that the total of our G&A costs last year equaled 15% of last year's direct operating costs.

Burdens are calculated because they simplify estimating when cost projections are made. They may be applied on the basis of person-hours or direct dollar costs. Of course, they are applied based on an estimate of the number of hours or direct dollars that will be spent this year, or for a particular project. If the actual number of direct hours or costs is significantly different, the burdens may well be inaccurate. For this reason, many government contracts call for post facto audits of all costs, with burdens to be adjusted based on actual costs all the way around.

From a manager's standpoint, these overhead factors are called burdens because they have the effect of raising the level of costs that must be covered by an activity or product in the company. It is not good enough just to cover the direct costs of the effort; one must also generate enough revenue to contribute to the overhead costs That increases the burden on the manager, all right. That is why it is always a good idea to find out just what costs are and are not included in the burden calculations that are handed to you, rather than assuming that the number is unchangeable.

Sunk and Avoidable Costs

Sometimes all of this allocation gives us an inaccurate picture of what something is really going to cost us in dollars.

Our decision-making process has to take into account how much something may already have cost us, also stated as how much we have sunk into a project so far. If we are going to switch from Process A to Process

B, we calculate the costs of Process B. But a cost analysis of any possible shift must also include the decision of whether we are willing to write off the investment we have in Process A. Will going to Process B save enough money to offset that write-off?

Sunk costs are sunk; they're gone. The decision you are to make right now must be made on the basis of future costs and returns. Many companies have taken sunk costs into consideration, staying with Process A in our example because of all the money invested in it. There's a technical term for that approach: throwing good money after bad.

Another example of a sunk cost is an additional task to be assigned to an employee who is being paid for a minimum number of hours. It is possible that no "extra" cash outlay is involved here, because with the minimum payment, that labor cost may have already been incurred, whether or not the additional task is performed.

Similarly, if we stop doing something, the "allocated cost" breakdown is an unreliable guide to our real potential cost savings. Even if we drive our car fewer miles, we still have the monthly car payment. The only costs we avoid by driving less are gasoline, tolls, perhaps oil and some fluids, and some wear and tear on tires and other things. Those are the avoidable costs. Other, fixed costs remain, and these will then have to be reallocated over the lower number of miles driven. Think about that for a minute: As incredible as it may sound, driving fewer miles would increase our cost per mile of driving!

Out-of-Pocket Costs

Sometimes, cost calculations for proposed projects are made based just on the actual expenditures that will have to be made to carry out the project, without regard to all the allocated costs involved. In our automotive example above, we might say that the out-of-pocket cost of a trip involves the gasoline that we purchase. For a railroad, they may just consider the direct costs of adding a train; wages, fuel, and so on. After all, the tracks are there already.

Sometimes a look at out-of-pocket costs can help a manager toward a decision to do, or not to do, something new. The question is, If we can add $10 to our revenue by increasing our out-of-pocket costs by $5, should we do it? Generally, the answer is yes. Never mind the accountants telling us that allocated overhead costs are $6 and we would "lose money." We have already spent the overhead costs. Remember, we're not looking at average costs, with all allocations; we're looking at the marginal cost, or the cost of making the next unit.

There's another problem in organizations that revere sunk costs: the pressure to use a second-rate system or machine "because we already own it." When word processors and personal computers came into vogue, many professional people in consulting firms discovered that their report-writing time was used more efficiently at the computer rather than with the old method of writing the draft on yellow legal pads, having it typed, reviewing and correcting it, and then having it retyped. In one firm (a vivid memory), not only were the professionals not encouraged to use this time-saving approach, but they were pressured to continue to use the centralized steno pool with its expensive (but slow) word-processor hardware. Why? Because "We have made a significant investment in this equipment. The cost of that equipment is in our overhead, and it must be used." Used, even if the total out-of-pocket cost (time) was greater. It took almost 2 years of widespread rebellion before the equipment was quietly retired.

Marginal Costs

The concept of marginal costs involves the cost of producing one more or one less unit than we are now doing. That unit is said to be at the end of the line, or "at the margin." What is the real cost of that last unit? As with revenues, the marginal cost is not the same as the average cost.

In general, as we increase our output, the per-unit costs drop, because we experience some economies of scale. Not only are we likely to have lower variable costs because of more efficient production, but in addition, fixed costs are allocated over a larger number of units, which lowers the total unit cost.

But if we were to keep on increasing output, we would eventually begin to strain, to reach the point at which producing that next unit would cost more than producing the one just before it. That's because of overtime, added coordination time, plant crowding, materials becoming less available or more expensive, and so on. Even though we may still make a profit, we would make increasingly lower profits on each unit made under such a strain. And we would eventually come to a point where the cost of making that next widget is greater than the revenue to be derived from selling it. How that creates a second breakeven point is covered in the next chapter. Figure 7.4 shows the relationship between marginal revenue and marginal cost.

The marketing manager must be aware that the push to produce more and more goods can actually be harmful to the company. Higher production quantities do not automatically produce higher profits.

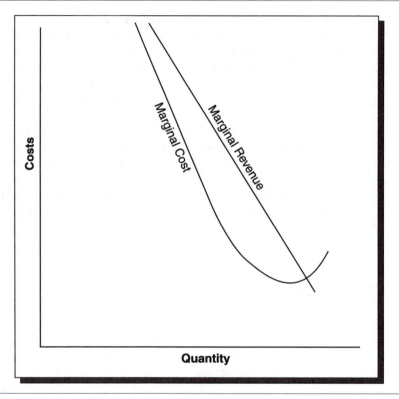

Figure 7.4   Marginal Costs

Inventory and Stockturn

Inventory of products depends on what kind of business we have. Many retailers buy their stock of goods and sell it virtually unchanged. They have one kind of inventory, for goods to be sold.

A manufacturer, on the other hand, has three types of inventory.

1. There is a *materials inventory* of raw materials and purchased components waiting to be worked on.

2. As the materials are drawn from stock and are worked on to fabricate our product, the cost of the labor involved is added to the base material cost, because the labor is adding value to the raw material. At any given time, a certain amount of our unfinished product will be a *work in process inventory*, with its value being the total of materials and labor costs, along with other direct costs, accumulated thus far.

3. When products are finished but not yet sold, they reside in a *finished goods inventory*, valued at their total accumulated cost of materials, labor, and overhead. Note that they are not valued at their hoped-for sale price but at their calculated cost.

Our inventory started as an accumulation of costs related to raw materials and labor, or goods for resale. But now look: Those costs are not expenses; they have been magically transformed. The inventory, or the total of our three inventories, has become a current asset, not an expense: increase (Debit) inventory, decrease (Credit) cash, as we pay the bills.

Three items bear consideration here: first, the real value of the inventory, second, the value of having it, and third, its velocity.

Theoretically, a company could produce goods continuously, and even if none were ever sold, the value of the inventory asset would increase as long as the firm had money to spend on producing product. That would make the asset side of a Balance Sheet apparently better, although the Income Statement would not be much to look at.

Although that idea is silly, what's not silly is that some of the items in our inventories may actually be close to worthless on the market, regardless of what they cost us. Obsolete products, damaged products, and questionable products all take up space. Companies periodically review their inventories, including making physical counts to verify what the ledgers say about how much is there. On the basis of that count and decisions made about questionable items, stuff will be disposed of and a downward adjustment will be made to remove the costs of the discarded material from the inventory's value. In the vernacular, we call that "writing off" part of the inventory.

That write-off is a cost, an expense: decrease (Credit) Inventory, Increase (Debit) Scrappage Expense. The expense that is written off therefore reduces profits. The question is, Is it an operating expense or an extraordinary expense? That's important to managers of the operation, because they will be judged on operating results. If the inventory adjustment is considered and decided to be an extraordinary expense, it will not be subtracted from operating profits and the managers will have turned in a better performance. The reason for the write-off may play a large role in where the cost is placed: If the write-off was caused by decisions beyond the operating managers' area of responsibility, it is less likely to affect them. But if they don't understand how write-offs work, they could be damaged and never know why.

On the other hand, we might also appear to be profiting from our inventory, because the value of some material we bought has gone up since we bought it. Photographers have suddenly found this with film containing silver, for example.

Well, sorry; the rule (and this one is a tax law) is that inventories are to be valued at "cost or market, whichever is lower." The gain on materials that increase in value will not show in inventory valuations. It will be recognized (and taxed) at the time of the sale. Sometimes, there is indeed hidden treasure in undervalued inventories, which tempts corporate raiders.

The value of having the inventory is, of course, the ability to satisfy the customer. That means having what customers want, when they want it. Because maintaining an inventory costs money (storage expense plus capital cost of having the goods), there is a continuing trade-off between cost reduction by reducing inventory and the negative consequence of not having the items on hand when the customers need them.

Marketing people generally want to minimize stockouts, which do not satisfy customers, whereas others in the firm seek efficiency. They discount or disregard the cost of a stockout because lost revenue is more difficult to measure. The conflict is usually best settled by replacing theory with fact, analyzing actual and projected customer demand, and adjusting the contents of our inventory to suit. This also may sound obvious, but I have seen instances of stockouts in Atlanta while Denver had an abundance of the same item. Denver had an abundance because it was an Atlanta customer who was the largest user, whereas a large Denver customer had moved to San Diego 5 years previously.

Like prices, the best inventories are customer driven and continuously monitored.

With regard to velocity, we are interested in the *stockturn rate*. Stockturn is calculated by dividing the Cost of Goods Sold, or Cost of Sales (see the Income Statement) for the year, by the average inventory during the year. Note that an approximation of the average inventory is also available on the Income Statement, because in calculating Cost of Goods Sold, we used the opening and closing inventories. If we add the opening and closing inventories together and divide by 2, we get an average inventory.

Now, how many times in a year do we turn over that average inventory? The higher that number is, the less dust gathers on our merchandise and the less money we spend on the capital and storage costs of maintaining that inventory.

A good stockturn rate varies from industry to industry and from product to product. A boutique store or boat dealer may be doing well at an annual stockturn rate of 1 or 2 times, whereas a grocery store might expect 10 to 12 turns for pet food and detergents and 60 to 180 stockturns for fresh fruits and vegetables (every 2 to 6 days). Obviously, the boutique charges a higher price to cover the costs of its larger and slower-moving inventory.

LIFO and FIFO

While we're on inventory, this may be a good time to try to explain LIFO and FIFO, two acronyms that we see but may not understand. They have to do with how our inventory is valued, and are a good example of how cagey human decisions can alter the value of what seems obvious.

Assume that we have 100 widgets in inventory and that they were not all purchased at the same time or at the same price. Assume further that the ones we bought more recently were purchased at a higher price than the ones we bought earlier. That's not too far from reality in our economy.

Now, as we remove widgets from our inventory to process and sell them, which widgets do we remove first? The ones we bought first, or the ones we bought last? Is it First In, First Out (FIFO), or Last In, First Out (LIFO)?

The difference can be important to our costs. Although it may seem straightforward to say that what we bought first should go out first, we soon find that tax considerations make us less straightforward. If we use the earlier widgets, with their lower value, then our profit per widget is higher than if we used the last, more expensive widgets we bought. Lower expense means our calculated profit and therefore our taxes are also higher, and that's why the LIFO method came into being. In fact, many companies use FIFO for internal purposes (to make the profit look as good as possible) and LIFO for tax purposes (to make the taxes as low as possible). How can they do that? By keeping two sets of books, that's how. Keeping two sets of books is not illegal.

A Cost Control Fallacy

One of the more insidious dangers in organizations is the mindless approach to cost control often practiced by administrative people whose focus is very short. In many cases, a saving can actually cost more than it saves. The following extreme but actual example makes the point:

It's a case of unthinking sabotage in the mail room. A customer had requested information about a product right away. The salesperson was told, "It's between you and Company X, and we're about to make the decision." The salesperson put together a package with the requested information to be sent out, quickly. *Tout de suite*. Right Now.

The precious package went to the mail room. Three days later, the salesperson followed up with the customer, only to be told that the package had not yet arrived. The salesperson put together another package, got in his car, and drove it out that morning to the customer, located 90 minutes away. By doing so, he saved the sale and got the order. Two weeks later, the customer contact called and told the salesperson that the original package had arrived that day; it had been sent third class.

After the salesperson descended from the ceiling, he visited the mail room. He had asked for priority shipment. The mail room clerk showed the salesperson a memo from the administrative manager, who oversaw the mail room. The memo essentially stated that to reduce mailing costs, any envelope weighing more than 4 ounces was to be sent third class. The salesperson's next visit was to his boss, the sales manager, who tried to set the administrative manager straight. It took 60 days and the intervention of the CEO before the administrative manager grudgingly allowed the Sales Department to "waste" money sending stuff out first class, even to potential customers.

And did the administrative manager learn anything from this? Did he see any lights at all? Well, he actually tried to get his revenge: When he reviewed the salesperson's expense report, he questioned the mileage incurred by the salesperson to deliver the package, asking that it be disallowed as "unnecessary, because there were less expensive alternate means of delivery available."

I bring this up because it's a perfect example of a missed focus: internal cost reduction versus customer satisfaction.

Fun with Depreciation and Amortization

There is one other basic classification of costs: Are they *expenses* or are they *capital costs*? The definitions are as follows:

An *expense* is an expenditure of dollars for a cost that will be incurred in the present year. Examples are payroll, telephone bills, client lunches, and so on.

A *capital cost* is an expenditure of dollars for an item that will have a life longer than 1 year. For example, buildings, automobiles, and factory machinery. When the life of an asset is longer than 1 year, the accountants set up a depreciation table to allocate a portion of the total cost (minus the scrap value) to each year of the asset's life. A $120,000 machine with an estimated life of 10 years and a scrap value of $20,000 would be written off as an expense at the rate of $10,000 per year if "straight line" depreciation is used.

There are many methods of charging depreciation. There are also many methods of allocating or amortizing other multiyear expenses. For example, how do we account for the cost of developing a product? So much per year? So much per item sold? So much per hundred dollars of revenue received? So much per hundred dollars of profit generated? It's not obvious, is it? Consider each of those approaches. Each has its advantages and disadvantages, and each approach will have its advocates and detractors in the company. The method used will be the one that is approved.

In the case of depreciation, as limited by law, the lifetime, the scrap value, what goes into the original cost figure, and the method used for depreciation are all estimates approved by the boss. They are not immutable numbers arrived at by scientific means.

That's important, because the company's assets are all charged to and allocated among the company's activities. That means your operation has costs charged to it for things you never see. If you think the charging of senior executive time to a consulting project described in Chapter 2 is bad, consider all the possible allocations that could be charged to you. The trouble is that (a) you may be unaware that these allocations are being made or (b) you take them for granted, thinking that they are unchangeable.

So, we find things like costs of a Washington government relations office allocated to operations that have no relationship to the Washington office, or equipment costs allocated to departments that never use that equipment. My favorite was a textbook replacement cost allocation levied on the divisions of a college, based on each division's total expense budget. The broadcasting division in that college used no textbooks, but they were charged for them because they were "a division of the College." Only after considerable effort was the inappropriate charge removed. It will pay you to research and understand every cost allocation made on your operation and to argue for fairness, accuracy, and justice. You can bet that the system got the way it is because others successfully made such arguments in years past.

Can We Really Measure Advertising Costs?

George Washington Hill, the legendary CEO of the American Tobacco Company in the 1930s, was often quoted as saying, "I know that half of my advertising budget is wasted; I just don't know which half."

Of all the expenses in an organization, advertising is usually most vulnerable to the cost-cutter's knife. The reason is found in the oversimplification that underlies Mr. Hill's glib statement. Many managers, faced with the inability to establish a direct, clear relationship between advertising and sales or profit, assume that measurement is impossible. Also, advertising expense is controllable; there's no government requirement or guideline, and cutting advertising is not likely to cause labor unrest. So, let's cut the fuzzy budget item.

The situation has not been helped by advertising people who base their successes on creativity and presentation skills rather than results. Still, techniques for measuring advertising effectiveness have come a long way since Mr. Hill's day.

Take for example, the simple decision, Should we advertise in Magazine A or Magazine B? First, let's accept that the decision should be based on something more substantial than "I feel better about Magazine A; it's the one I read."

If Magazine A charges $1,200 for a full-page ad and has 240,000 readers, then its cost per thousand (CPM) readers is $5, or $1,200/240. If Magazine B charges $1,500 and has 320,000 readers, the CPM is $4.69. But part of the calculation has to include your estimate of the relationship between the magazine's readership and your target audience. Despite its higher readership, Magazine B may not be the better investment. If only half of Magazine B's 320,000 readers fall within your target market group, the effective CPM doubles to $9.38. If 75% of Magazine A's circulation, or 180,000 readers, are within your target group, the effective CPM is $1,200/180, or $6.67. Magazine A is the better buy.

The same formula can also be applied to trade show booths and can even be modified by adjusting for the probability of purchasers or decision makers being in attendance, rather than mere lookers. In other words, trade show attendees are not necessarily potential customers. The best probability figures are derived from our own experience, which is why we ask customers, "How did you hear about us?"

Eight

Strategy: Breakeven and Profitability

Profit Is Why We're Here

To say that we're here to make a profit may seem obvious, but there are still those people who believe that profits are somehow inherently evil. They are not. Profit and, more important, the hope of profit, make up the engine that is the greatest motivator ever known. Any profit we earn comes because we have satisfied enough customers to earn it. Review with me for a moment two of the definitions from Chapter 1:

Profit: The amount by which our customers believe our products to be worth more than the resources we expended on those products.

Loss: The amount by which present and potential customers believe our products to be worth less than the resources we expended on those products.

The customers have ultimate control over the situation.

We have already seen that increased sales do not necessarily bring about increasing profits, for two reasons. First, at some point, as we increase production, the marginal cost per unit will rise. Second, marginal revenue (the revenue derived from that next unit) will fall, because of demand curves. To sell a larger quantity, we must charge a lower price. At some point, that becomes counterproductive.

85

That's the economic view. The economists, accountants, and finance people all have one thing in common in their approaches to the business and its measurement: All three take customers and sales for granted, or look at them in the abstract.

Sales and Profits

Many managers, particularly those who have come up through the sales ranks, have focused on sales, on revenues, assuming that where sales rise, rising profits are sure to follow. Sometimes, the pressure to increase sales actually lowers profits. To get the business (to increase sales), we tend to cut our prices and make deals for certain customers, lowering our profit.

The result is that our "best" customer—the one who buys the highest volume of goods or services from us—may not be our actual best customer at all, in terms of profit. We have to figure the cost of the special prices, the favors, the little (and big) extras that tend to flow to the high-volume customer. A profitability analysis by customer can yield hair-raising results.

The sales force itself can be a cause of lower profits, but they are not to blame. Are they continuously pushing for higher sales volumes, regardless of profitability? Who can blame them, because their commissions are based on sales volume.

Too many companies operate compensation packages that reward behavior that lowers the company's profit. Clearly, a better sales compensation package involves some element related to profit, not just volume.

The result is expansion, but it is not necessarily growth. As anyone who is on a diet can tell you, expansion and growth are not the same thing. To have growth, there must be profit to finance it. If we are to attract capital for our project, there must be profit or the hope of profit.

Most often, we are judged by our Return on Assets or Return on Equity (including all of those costs allocated to us) during a period of time. Exactly how that period of time is defined can be a hurdle in itself. Will we have enough time to achieve a level of sales where revenues cover the costs?

Breaking Even

Our first consideration, before looking at profit levels, is avoiding a loss, that is, Breaking Even, or Achieving a Condition in Which Revenues Exceed Expenses.

We have already looked at the cost curve, in Figure 7.1. Now, let's add a revenue curve, to create Figure 8.1. The revenue curve is curved to reflect diminishing revenue at higher quantities, and the cost curve curves to reflect increasing costs as production increases.

The curves intersect for the first time at the breakeven point. A sales level below that quantity means that not enough revenue will be generated to cover costs. Above that level, we will generate revenue in excess of costs. That's breakeven.

But look! The lines cross again, out to the right. And by now you have figured out that if we sell a quantity up in that range, we had better be prepared to lose money again. We would have been too successful for our own good.

There is a maximum profit point: the point at which the vertical distance between total revenue and total cost curves is the greatest. Because

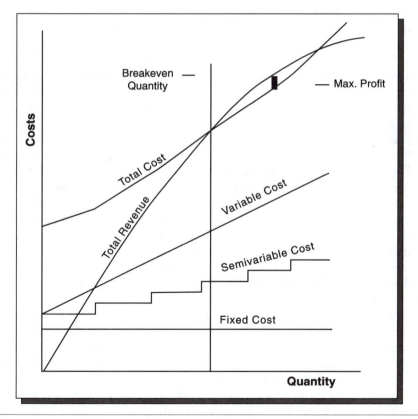

Figure 8.1   Breakeven Points

you are not likely to have enough information about customer demand to hit it exactly, it's comforting to know that there is a range of profitability on either side of it.

By the way, we are also looking at the main reason why so many business plans get laughed at. All too often, the projections in them contain linear projections; the assumption is that "good things will keep on happening forever." It's a fallacy, but it's a comfortable fallacy, and one that's easy to understand, and so many people indulge in it.

Fixed Costs and Profitability

Let's take a look at the difference in probability brought about by the relative proportion of fixed costs and variable costs in our production process. Take a look at these two charts, Figures 8.2a and 8.2b.

In Figure 8.2a, the total cost of the process involves relatively low fixed costs and a high proportion of variable costs, usually labor. Figure 8.2b shows a situation in which capital invested in machinery and other facilities has reduced the portion of variable-cost labor in each unit produced.

Perhaps the best example involves Johannes Gutenberg, inventor of movable type for printing. Before Gutenberg, books were written by hand. The historic image is that of monks carefully inscribing pages using quill pens. That's Figure 8.2a. Low fixed costs; tables, chairs, quills. But the labor component of the cost is very high. Only religious fervor, in the case of the monks, kept labor costs from going through the roof. But still, books were expensive, available only to a small part of the population.

Enter Herr Gutenberg. A producer of books now could make a fixed-cost investment in a wide array of movable-type letters, along with the printing press into which the blocks of letters would fit, once arranged into paragraphs. This meant that although the cost of the first copy of the book to be printed still involved the labor of setting type in trays, setting up the printing press, and running off a copy, the cost of the second copy, and all copies thereafter, involved only the cost of running off another copy, a very small fraction of the total cost.

Now look again at Figures 8.2a and 8.2b and you'll see why people make fixed-cost investments to reduce the variable cost per unit produced. After reaching the break-even point, we begin to show a profit. How much of a profit we make is represented graphically by the difference in the slopes of the Total Revenue and Total Cost curves. The faster the revenue and cost lines diverge, or the greater the angle between the two lines, the greater the profitability. And, as we can see, Figure 8.2b, with the higher fixed-cost investment, shows a greater rate of profit after

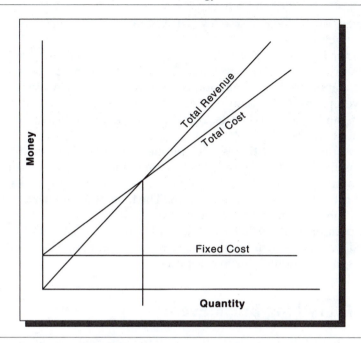

Figures 8.2a   Low Fixed Costs

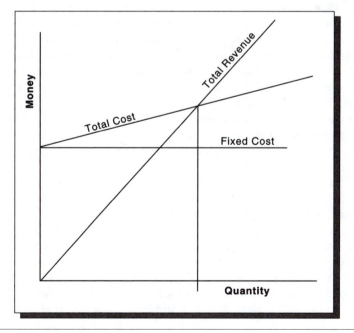

Figures 8.2b   High Fixed Costs

breakeven. We make more money faster. Sometimes, we make much more money much faster.

Whether it's books, manhole covers, or computer chips, if the manufacturer invests in machinery that allows more items to be produced with less labor per item, profitability increases. The downside is that the breakeven production quantity point will be higher because of the need to cover the higher fixed costs. But if the market is there, the fixed-cost investment will be made.

The best example of this is a telephone company. Once the fixed-cost system is in place, the variable cost of each additional telephone call is almost nothing. As we know, the revenue is somewhat more than nothing and is based on the number of calls. The telephone breakeven point is high, but once it is met, the profit is great.

Competition being what it is, the ultimate result is that if costs are driven down, prices will follow. We have seen that happen with all kinds of goods, from automobiles to computers.

Must Everything Break Even?

A danger to watch out for is the tendency to microanalyze each and every product item in the company's line. Accountants love to do this because it makes them look thorough. The mantra goes, "If there's a product in our line that's not breaking even, get it up or get it out!"

Terrific. Except that we're back to the customer's perceptions again. And the customer may be persuaded to buy one product in our line because we have a full line of products. A few years ago, I had the pleasure of creating a series of public transit express bus services from a well-known downtown area to various suburbs. The service was based on market research rather than political expediency. We charged a premium fare, offered premium service, and we filled most of the buses. And, most gratifyingly, the taxpayer subsidy per passenger on these expresses was far lower than the average subsidy (loss) for the system.

Essentially, we had downtown evening express departures at 5:05, 5:10, 5:15, 5:25, and 6:00 p.m. When I say we filled most of the buses, I mean that the 6:00 departure usually left downtown less than a third full. The earlier buses were packed. So, the accountants did the analysis and showed that the 6:00 trip was losing money. The planners urged its elimination. But your friendly marketing director argued against such a cut. That 6:00 trip was the safety valve that caused people to use the express service in the first place. Customers knew that if they worked a bit late and missed the 5:25 trip, they would not be stranded downtown. We had to take a relative loss on the 6:00 trip to make the entire express service work.

The position was vindicated a couple of years later, after I and my well-trained successor had moved on. The planners and accountants did not go away; they eventually won, and the loser 6:00 p.m. trip was eliminated. Ridership on the other trips fell dramatically, making all of them less profitable. Of course, the planners' first reaction was to recommend eliminating those earlier trips too, now that they were less profitable. Then somebody remembered the lessons of marketing, and the 6:00 p.m. trip was restored. With that reassurance that they would not be trapped, riders returned.

Nine

Cash

Cash Flow

You may have heard people say, "We're making money, but we have a cash flow problem." That's a more common occurrence than most of us would like to believe. The surprise usually is that you can indeed be making money, that is, showing a profit on the Income Statement, and yet not have enough cash to pay the bills.

A company that cannot pay its bills will soon be out of business. A company that falls behind in paying its bills will be regarded with suspicion and will have difficulty obtaining credit. The lack of credit will further aggravate a cash flow problem, because more cash will have to be paid out even sooner. Word travels very fast about bad credit news. Your primary suppliers will become cautious, perhaps even refuse to ship to you until they are paid. They may increase their prices or limit the quantities of goods they will ship to you.

So, just at the time orders for your products, that is, sales, are increasing, you find that your ability to fill those orders is being constricted. If that constriction keeps you from meeting your delivery commitments, that negatively affects your revenue and your relationships with your customers.

Inadequate cash flow can be a downward death spiral for a business.

We'll return to cash flow in a bit. First, let's look at why cash is not necessarily income and vice versa.

Source and Use of Funds

The first thing we have to realize is that there is a considerable difference between the Income Statement showing the results of our operations, and the progress of cash into and out of our company. The accountants have developed a way to keep track of cash.

In addition to the Balance Sheet and the Income Statement, a third statement is prepared by company accountants to account for the flow of cash into and out of the organization. That report is called the Statement of Source and Use of Funds. A simplified example appears as Figure 9.1.

The Funds Statement tells us where the money came from and where it went during the year. We have developed a comparative statement for 2 years, which is a not uncommon form of presentation.

Basically, there are only five places from which a company gets cash:

1. Profit from operations

2. Cash advances from clients and others

3. Sale of assets

4. Loans

5. Capital investment

On the other hand, there are only five areas in which a company spends cash:

1. Loss from operations

2. Deposits and advance payments made

3. Purchase of assets

4. Repayment of loans

5. Dividends to owners

Now, let's look at the Bilgewater statement.

Sources of Funds

Profit Before Taxation or, *Net Income Before Taxes,* is the net operating profit from the Income Statement. But some adjustments need to be made to the profit figure, because there are items in the Income Statement that, although they affect profit, may not affect cash. The first of these is Depreciation. *Depreciation* is a noncash expense. It's the portion of the value of our plant and equipment that we have elected to charge off to this year's

Bilgewater Beverage Company
Statement of Source and Use of Funds
For the Year Ending December 31, 2004

(Cash Flow)

	2003	2004
Source of Funds		
Profit Before Taxation	970,000	1,030,000
Adjustment for Items Not Involving the Movement of Funds:		
Depreciation	340,000	320,000
Profit on disposal of fixed assests	(7,000)	(2,000)
Total Funds Generated From Operations	1,303,000	1,348,000
Funds From Other Sources		
Cash advances	4,000	7,000
Cash from sales of fixed assets	67,000	32,000
Proceeds from loans	25,000	102,000
Cash from investments	3,000	4,000
Total Nonoperating Funds Generated	99,000	145,000
Total Funds From All Sources	1,402,000	1,493,000
Application of Funds		
Dividend paid	320,000	320,000
Tax paid	640,000	670,000
Purchase of fixed assets	161,000	720,000
Investments made	7,000	22,000
Loan repayments	10,000	--
Advances and deposits	30,000	50,000
Total Funds Applied	1,168,000	1,782,000
Cash in Cash Balance	234,000	(289,000)

Figure 9.1   Source and Use of Funds Statement

production; that is, we have elected to deduct this amount from the value of the assets and charge it as an expense. Although we showed it as an expense, no cash left the property. So, we must add depreciation to the Net Profit figure, because we still have the cash.

We also sold some fixed assets, and we took a loss on them. The proceeds from the sale show up under Funds from Other Sources, but because it is a loss, it is deducted from our profit for the year. The result of the adjustments gives us *Total Funds Generated From Operations*.

Bilgewater also got cash from places other than operations. Customers advanced some cash for items not yet delivered; we have the money, but not the sale. Think of a magazine subscription. You pay for a year's worth of magazines in advance. The publisher has the cash advance, but should not carry a sale until each month's issue is sent to you. (Some publishers do credit a sale early, which distorts their figures.)

We have already covered the *Sales of Fixed Assets*. Here is where the proceeds of a sale are recorded.

Proceeds From Loans refers to money that Bilgewater borrowed each year; the cash they received when they signed the papers is shown here.

Cash From Investments is money received from Bilgewater's investments. Many financial officers use short-term interest-bearing investments to earn money on cash that would otherwise be idle. Some companies have extensive investment portfolios, including subsidiary companies. Money received from those sources is shown here.

Application of Funds

Dividend Paid refers to cash that was paid out to the owners this year in the form of a dividend on their stock.

Tax Paid is recorded here, to show the expenditure.

Purchase of Fixed Assets is money spent now to buy items of plant and equipment that will be depreciated over a period of time.

Investments Made is the total of money that Bilgewater invested in non-operating areas this year.

Loan Repayments are deducted here. Although Bilgewater borrowed money, they also reduced some loan balances. The reductions are shown here.

Advances and Deposits represents funds expended by Bilgewater before delivery of goods or services.

The net result is the change in Bilgewater's *cash position* during the year. We should note that although Bilgewater's profit was up this year, their cash position was down, likely because they purchased a larger amount of assets. Consider this a reminder that profit and cash can (and often do) move in opposite directions.

Receivables and Payables: A/R and A/P

Our Balance Sheet shows the company's Accounts Receivable and Accounts Payable. The Income Statement shows Sales and Cost of Goods Sold.

Let's look at our friends at Bilgewater Beverage Company, whom we remember from the Income Statement (Figure 3.2) in Chapter 3.

The statement shows:

Net Sales	$7,050,000
Goods Available for Sale	3,800,000
Cost of Goods Sold	3,580,000
Beginning Inventory	440,000
Ending Inventory	220,000
Total Operating Expenses	2,700,000
Depreciation	320,000

The Balance Sheet (Figure 3.1) in Chapter 3 shows:

Accounts Receivable	$550,000
Accounts Payable	290,000

These numbers allow us to make a few calculations applicable to this section and the next section.

Those calculations are important to us as marketing managers because they provide an estimate of the credit of a present or potential customer. We have to understand the probability that we will, in fact, get paid for the goods and services we provide.

Normal credit terms in business involve payment in 30 days. That is, payment is due 30 days after the goods are received by the buyer. Some customers may pay sooner, some later. How well a company does in collecting on its receivables affects its financial health. The accountants and financial analysts speak in terms of the "age of receivables," or how old they are or how long the time is from delivery to payment.

Well, what's the age of Bilgewater Beverage's receivables? We can make a rough calculation by taking the Accounts Receivable and dividing by the Net Sales ($550,000/7,050,000 = 0.078). So Bilgewater's receivables are just under 8% of sales. Eight percent of 365 days in a year (365 × 8% or 365 × 0.08 = 29.2 days) is a little less than a month. So, the customers are mostly paying within 30 days. Bilgewater is quite likely on top of its collections, and some customers are likely paying in advance.

Now for the age of the payables. Here we match Accounts Payable against the Cost of Goods Sold and compare that to the fraction of a 365-day year ($290,000/3,580,000 = 8.1 percent); 365 days × 8.1% = 29.6 or 30 days. Bilgewater is paying its bills substantially on time.

If the number of days in either case had substantially exceeded 30, some questions would arise. If the customers are taking a long time to pay, somebody needs to monitor collections more closely. But that's not just to hound people; we need to understand the situation with that customer.

Do late payments occur because of disputes between buyer and seller? Or is late payment a conscious strategy? Some companies deliberately pay slowly, because they believe that delaying payment reduces the cash, or working capital, they need to operate. It's a thin line, because abuse of credit can cause suppliers to raise their prices or to demand cash payment, either of which will offset the savings gained by foot-dragging.

It might be useful to look at this picture in terms of a cash gap.

Cash Flows and Cash Gaps

The problem we have is financing the cash gap. This is the period of time that we must have money to cover between the date we pay for things and the day we get paid.

A peanut vendor at a football game may buy $50 worth of peanuts at wholesale, which he will sell for $100 retail during the game. If he buys and pays for the peanuts on the morning of the game and sells at least half of what he bought (to bring in at least $50), his cash gap is about 5 hours. On the other hand, if he didn't actually have to pay his supplier for the peanuts until after the game, he has no cash gap at all.

Most companies are not so lucky. Yes, all of us would like to be paid for our goods before we have to pay our suppliers, but most of the time it doesn't work out that way. If we have normal trade credit, we pay for goods we receive 30 days after we receive them. The goods will languish in inventory for some period of time and then will be sold. Our customers will pay for the goods 30 days after delivery to them; maybe they will pay more than 30 days after. Although there is money coming in, a great deal of it is chasing money that we have already spent.

It follows that we can reduce our cash gap by (a) reducing the length of time items stay in our inventory or increasing the stockturn rate, (b) making sure that our customers pay as soon as possible, or (c) not paying our suppliers quite as promptly. As we noted earlier, choice (c) is likely to have adverse consequences, such as removal of credit, which would suddenly lengthen the cash gap by 30 days.

We have already looked at two of the factors that affect the cash gap: the length of receivables and the length of payables. In our Bilgewater Beverage example, receivables wait 26 days before payment and payables wait 30 days.

There's one more factor in the cash gap, and that's the velocity of the inventory, or stockturn. You will remember that the stockturn rate is calculated by dividing Cost of Goods Sold ($3,580,000) by the average inventory. Bilgewater's average inventory is $330,000 (Beginning Inventory of $440,000 + Ending Inventory of $220,000, divided by 2).

Bilgewater's stockturn rate thus is $3,580,000/330,000 = 10.8. This is not a percentage; it indicates that the average inventory turns over 10.8 times a year. We divide the year by 11 (no, not 10.8; dividing by 11 is close enough!) to get the number of days that goods wait in inventory. That's 33.2 or 33 days. Increasing the velocity of inventory or stockturn will reduce the number of days in the cash gap and will reduce the cash requirement.

How long, in days, is the cash gap?

When we receive goods, two time lines begin to run simultaneously. The first time line counts the days until we pay for the goods. The second time line counts the days that the goods remain in inventory and then adds the days before the customer pays for the goods.

So, Bilgewater pays for its goods an average of 30 days after they arrive; that's our first time line. On the second time line, the goods are in inventory for an average of 33 days, and the customers pay an average of 26 days after a sale. The total of our second time line is 59 days (33 + 26).

The number of days in the cash gap is the difference between our two time lines, in this case, 59 days − 30 days, or 29 days.

Let's put that another way: We need enough cash, often called *working capital*, to keep the business going for 29 days. And that assumes no increase in the level of sales during that time. If we're projecting and hoping for increased sales, we will need additional working capital.

How much cash do we need to have in order to finance the cash gap? In this example, we need to calculate the total required cash to cover 29 days' worth of operation.

We know that 29 days is about 8% of the 365 days in a year; that's sufficient precision for our purposes. The accountants will calculate it to the dollar; the marketing folks don't need all that detail.

Eight percent of our Cost of Goods Sold ($3,580,000) is $286,400.

Our total cash operating expenses for the year (not including depreciation) are $2,380,000 ($2,700,000 − $320,000). Eight percent of that is $190,400.

Those two figures add up to $476,800.

Bilgewater needs to have at least $476,800 in working capital to finance its present level of operations. That can be either invested capital or borrowed money, but that's what it needs to have.

Look at Bilgewater's Balance Sheet (Figure 3.1). As it happens, they do have cash and receivables in excess of that amount, but more cash would be welcome. If that amount of money were not present, Bilgewater would soon have a cash flow problem. And here is where expanding companies get into trouble: If the company is in an expanding market, with daily sales increasing, a cash pinch will come sooner and will be more severe, because average daily sales will be increasing. They will need more money to cover the costs of fulfilling the increased sales. That's the paradox that bedevils companies that cannot finance their expansion; they grow too fast. That is why you hear about companies that went bankrupt or were taken over by others in the middle of spectacularly rising sales; they could not finance the growth or did not understand the amount of money they would need to fund that growth.

Net Present Value

It probably does not surprise you to learn that a dollar received today is worth more than a dollar received a year from now. What may surprise you is the degree by which their values are different. As many people who owe money have found to their dismay, compound interest has a way of adding up faster than we expect. At a 10% interest rate, a given amount invested today will double in less than 7 years. At 6%, it takes a little less than 10 years.

If we look at that backwards, if someone offers you the choice of receiving $20,000 7 years from now or $10,000 today, which is better? Well, if you can invest $10,000 at a 10% compound interest rate, you'll have $21,436 in 7 years. If the rate of interest is only 8%, taking the $20,000 later means you'll be about $10 ahead; almost a wash. At a 6% interest rate, it would take almost 11 years for that $10,000 to reach $20,000. Let's not even consider those higher double-digit credit card interest rates.

The general rule is, money today is worth more than money in the future. That's the basis of net present value calculations.

Oh, by the way: If a state lottery pays off a million dollars at $50,000 per year for 20 years, they never have a million dollars tied up. All they have to do is put $833,334 in an account that bears 6% interest. If they can get 8% interest, the amount they need to invest to pay a winner his or her "million" is only $625,000. Which is why, if you win, they don't like to give you the option of getting your million dollars now. They have a lower lump sum option. Take it.

Ten

Budgets

What Is a Budget?

What is a budget? A simple question, but one with a number of not-so-simple answers. Let's define the word *budget* first. Here are two definitions:

1. A budget is a plan for operating a business or project, based on estimates of future revenue and costs and used as a guide and control device. The numbers are estimates of the market and revenue and estimates of the resources we are expected to expend during a given time period to generate that estimated revenue. Because the budget elements are only estimates and targets, we are judged on our actual results relative to the budget. The criterion on which such a budget is judged is accuracy: How close did we come to our estimates? A small variance either way is not critical. A large variance either way, even favorable, requires an explanation, because it represents a surprise from which we may learn.

2. A budget is a plan for operating a business or project, based on estimates of future revenue and costs and used as a guide and control device. In the area of costs, the budget numbers are ceilings above which we must not and may not spend, regardless of conditions. Even a small unfavorable variance is cause for alarm and possible punishment. An appeals process may be in place for additional expenditures; it is unofficially called "the bed of hot coals" in the company.

So, in our language, a *budget* number can mean *target* or *ceiling*. These are two very different definitions, each with different implications and leading to different strategies. Definition 1 is likely to be found in more open environments, younger companies, and, frankly, more successful ones. That's because it recognizes the real world as the controlling element, not the internal budget. Definition 2 is more common, because it is simpler to manage.

The primary thing you have to know is this: Which definition is operative in your organization? The arena is littered with the lifeless bodies of those who were operating under one definition—usually 1—while others in the company operated under the other—usually 2. Worse, top management may think they are using definition 1, whereas the accounting or financial types translate the process into definition 2 on the way down the chain of command.

Basis for Budgets: Last Year, Percentage, or Zero?

Every budget, as it is constructed, is an estimate, by human beings, of future events and results. In plain terms, it's a guess. In plainer terms, it's a guess that is designed to place the guesser in the most favorable light. More accurately, it's an approved guess, modified and ratified by upper management.

But how do we arrive at our guess? Usually, by extrapolating from last year. This is like the army that trains to fight the previous war. But it's simple, easy to justify, and easy to manage.

If last year's numbers are not used, then how do we estimate for a budget? Let's look at the most vulnerable budget in any company, the promotion budget.

We know that the promotion budget is a critical area of any marketing mix. How much to spend on personal selling, mass selling, and sales promotion? Problem is, promotion budgets often appear less vital to the success of the organization to people outside the marketing area.

The most common method of calculating promotion budget figures is to use last year's numbers, adjusted or not. Adding or multiplying by a factor is easy but not all that likely to be accurate.

The second most common method is to use a percentage of sales, either last year's actual or sales projected for next year. This might be expressed in sales dollar terms or in sales unit terms (dollars per case, per thousand, or per ton). This is also seen as simple to do, which is why many companies do it. No real thought is required.

Percentage of sales budgeting has at least two flaws. First, it does not take into account the real and unique situation being faced at a given time. Second, under this system, promotion costs automatically go up and down with sales, totally overlooking the fact that more promotion, not less, may be needed if sales are down, in order to raise the sales level.

Some companies budget by matching expenditures with competitors, or at least using the same percentages as a competitor. Quite often, this is the justification for promotional expenditures: "They're doing X; so should we."

Some companies decide to set aside all uncommitted revenue for promotion, investing in marketing for greater sales and future profits. That's an aggressive expansion.

There is one more method—basing the budget on the task to be done—which I discuss next.

This approach involves what has come to be called the "zero-base budget," in which the estimates are based on next year's estimated activity without regard for what happened last year. It's also called the task method, or basing the budget on the job to be done.

Zero-base or task-based is more involved than tying the budget to a percentage or other "outside" number. Essentially, we must review every detail of the marketing plan and cost it out. The costs of each task are totaled to arrive at the overall budget figure. This approach requires a closer look at the activities to be undertaken next year, but let's face it—last year's numbers are still often used as guidelines.

The task objectives may be expressed in terms of sales, customers, new and repeat sales, geographic penetration, or other measurement. The budgets are thus based on our real plans, rather than arbitrary ratios, to ensure adequate resources for the work ahead.

The Fantasy Factor

There's another thing that happens to budgets during their preparation: the fantasy factor.

Spreadsheet software makes it easy to create a budget by extrapolating from last year or by using the spreadsheet's macro functions to extrapolate a percentage of sales into the future. A detailed budget printed out from a spreadsheet can be a thing of beauty. The drawback, which mars many business plans and budgets, is that there is no fantasy detector built into the software. As I said in another context, precision is not necessarily accuracy.

But a budget is an approved estimate, and therefore we must gain approval from someone. What often happens in less successful companies is that even when the marketing people carefully prepare a detailed task-based budget, their work is then cut down by upper management to some arbitrary level consistent with management's pet ratios or percentages (based on "experience," that is, "last year").

Cost Fudge and Revenue Cotton Candy

The first Eternal Truth of budgeting is that costs are easier to budget than revenues. The accountants can swarm over cost estimates, building them up block by block, advertisement by advertisement, paper clip by paper clip, and come out with a printout that looks very realistic. It may even *be* very realistic.

Now, what happens to that very precious realistic cost estimate? This depends in large part on the operative definition of a budget as discussed at the outset of this chapter. If the definition of budget is (2), with *ceiling* as the operative word, the costs will likely have been inflated by some fudge factor, because it is a mortal sin to be over budget and everybody will look for a cushion. In a company in which different levels of management each prepare budgets that are then consolidated at each successive higher level, the fudge content can become layered and quite large.

Of course, the costs were based on the work that needed to be done to achieve stated objectives. What about those objectives?

The weak spot in any business plan or budget is the revenue estimate. We are dealing with human nature, competition, and so on. The data are external to the company and therefore not as comfortable as the internally generated costs.

Simply put, there is no easy way to estimate revenue. But we know that some people are better at estimating revenue than others. I had the pleasure of working with an accountant who had a knack for putting together accurate revenue projections. He made it look easy. He also died "in harness," and it may be some testimony to his skill and judgment as well as his character that his funeral cortege contained 64 cars. After his passing, nobody else came close to his level of accuracy.

The moral of that story is, Look around to find someone who is able to estimate revenue accurately. Reward that person. And don't ask how he or she does it; the answer is likely to be "I don't really know."

Because revenues are estimated with less precision than costs, revenues are more likely to be second-guessed or altered to make an estimate look better.

We'll hear something like "Those revenue estimates aren't high enough. Bump 'em up by 10, 15%." The original estimates may have been realistic, but if you are not able to defend them, they will now be replaced by managerial blue sky to "look better," for which you will later be held responsible.

The only way to combat this kind of mindlessness is with detail. If revenue is expected to be X, show how it gets there as a result of the investment. This many advertising impressions, this many sales calls, and (even with zero base) this is the expected yield, based on our experience. If all you do is make a rough guess, prepare to have it replaced by somebody else's rough guess.

Don't Just Divide by 12

Assuming that some kind of understanding is reached about what a budget is, exactly, and what the numbers will be for next year, there are still problems having to do with variability during the budget period. Simply stated, most budgets are created on the assumption of no variability from day to day or even from month to month. Why? Because it's easier to put a budget together that way. In the least detailed sample case, we estimate that we will spend $60,000 on widgets next year and divide that annual number by 12 to get a $5,000 per month budget figure.

That approach works just fine if you are in a situation where you actually do issue a widget purchase order for $5,000 each and every month, come hell or high water, regardless of the actual fluctuations in the business. But most budget items do not work that way, because most businesses don't work that way. Every business has some kind of seasonal variation during a year. Most of the items in your budget will vary from month to month, week to week, or even day to day.

Let's look at our widgets. We may have budgeted $5,000 per month, but the actual expense may look more like this:

Month	Budget	Actual	Variance to Date	Year	YTD
January	$5,000	5,300	+300	5,300	+300
February	5,000	4,600	−400	9,900	−100
March	5,000	5,700	+700	15,600	+600
April	5,000	4,700	−300	20,300	+300
May	5,000	4,800	−200	25,100	+100
June	5,000	5,000	0	30,100	+100
Total	30,000	30,100			

What appears to have happened is that you are running over the widget budget for the first 6 months of the year. In March, you were running more than 10% over the widget budget, and a variance of that size will set off alarm bells in most places.

What really happened, of course, was that January and March are normally heavy months in your industry, and February and April are lighter months. Furthermore, the first half of the year is a bit busier because business falls off in the summer months of July and August. But your widget budget was put together by dividing the annual figure by 12, which does not reflect the actual widget purchase schedule. According to the budget, you were spending more than you should. By June, the unfavorable variance is very small, but people have had 5 months to worry by then.

The problem here is that what counts in your performance evaluation is not reality but the perception of those who read the computer printouts all year. As early as the January report, when the computer kicked out that $300 "unfavorable variance," others in the company began thinking about ways to help you with your cost overrun situation "before it gets out of hand." Especially after that red flag in March, reality for you is likely to become time spent responding to memos of concern and preparing a series of update reports to "keep us informed" about the current status of the "widget problem," and your plan for "solving" it. We know that there is no real problem, but you will be under scrutiny and will be spending much time reassuring others that there is no problem.

It gets worse. Some people in the company will continue to associate you with the possibility that there may have been a problem (your denials are obviously self-serving) long after the fact. In an extreme case, people who have never met you may make decisions about your future based on what they saw in the computer printout and what they were told by others who didn't understand the situation or who seek to profit at your expense: "Oh yes, the widget problem. Well, Jones's difficulty is that his first reaction to a problem is to insist that there is no problem. But with [our, my] help, Jones got his unfavorable variance down to $100 by June."

All because somebody took the easy way out and divided an annual figure by 12 to set a budget.

The moral of this story is simple: Make sure that your budget takes into account the realities of your business, and put the effort into refining your estimates as much as possible.

This is not the same thing as adding "fudge factors," which add comfort while reducing the value of the budget as a management tool.

Revenues and Strategy

It is important to note that revenues are affected much more than costs by seasonal or day-to-day variability. I have already said that revenues are the most difficult budget element to forecast. We can improve our estimate a bit by looking at the calendar. This is particularly true in businesses in which many customers make small purchases, creating many transactions on a given day.

Each month has a given number of weekdays in it, and that number is not consistent. It varies between 20 and 23 days, depending on where the weekends fall. Holidays also affect the number. This can mean that as much as a 15% variance is caused just by the calendar, not counting holidays. (Three days is 15% of 20 days.) Furthermore, people in some of your target markets may be more likely to buy at the beginning of a month rather than at the end of a month. If you analyze the purchasing patterns of your target customers over time, you will get a better handle on revenue projections.

There's another kind of day-to-day variance, too. In each year, there are usually 4 months that contain five occurrences of a given weekday rather than four. That is one third of the months. If Friday is your heavy day, it would help when budgeting to know which months in the budget year have five Fridays in them. What is the buying pattern of your customers?

All of this involves more detail, and more work, than guessing at an annual figure and dividing by 12. Your reward for that effort will be a more realistic estimate against which you can judge and will be judged.

Some marketers who are savvy in the ways of budgeting use a little stratagem. They make it a practice, after preparing an annual budget estimate, to shift the focus and the funds a bit. They don't change the annual total, but they shift some dollars to overestimate expenses and to underestimate revenues in the first part of a budget year, compensating in the latter part of the year to reach the estimated annual totals. If we adjusted our widget budget to reflect the estimated timing as well as the estimated total, the budget might look like this:

Month	Budget	Actual	Variance to Date	Year Variance	YTD
January	$ 5,400	5,300	−100	5,300	−100
February	4,800	4,600	−200	9,900	−300
March	5,500	5,700	+200	15,600	−100
April	4,800	4,700	−100	20,300	−200
May	5,000	4,800	−200	25,100	−400
June	5,000	5,000	0	30,100	400
Total	30,500	30,100			

Note that the actuals have not changed. What has changed is that we're budgeting $30,500 in the first half of the year (and $29,500 in the second half). Our annual total is unchanged. But with this more accurate budget, the reports for the first months of the year show a favorable budget variance. Instead of being monitored and fussed over, you are being congratulated, or at least left alone. That's not because you fudged the figures; it's because the budget is now a better estimate.

In the revenue area, it's the reverse: If you state an underestimated revenue in the first part of the year and the actuals are in line with your original (or "real") estimates, the result is a pleasant surprise that ripples through the company. The practical effect is that you are not playing catch-up for the first part of the year. You are also spared the hassle of being "helped with your problem," with its attendant scrutiny and extra reporting.

Eleven

Just Look at the "Sadistics"

At a very early point, statistics entered your life, and they're not going away. In fact, the moment you were born, you became a statistic, to be charted and analyzed by those who study people. Year of birth, sex, ethnic origin, place of birth, birthday, all serve to include you into, and at the same time to exclude you from, certain groups that the mathematicians call sets.

Statistics is the process, science, and art of collecting and interpreting data that can be expressed numerically. It attempts to discover and define the characteristics of a larger universe or population by analyzing a representative sample from that universe.

Statistics serves two purposes:

1. To improve our understanding of the universe involved and permit us to make better decisions

2. To improve our ability to persuade others toward our point of view

These purposes are all too easily confused.

Mean Stuff and Deviations

In fact, there are three different kinds of average: the mean, the median, and the mode. We'll look at each of them.

The *mean* is the result obtained by adding up all the values and dividing this total by the number of items in the list. That is the arithmetic "average."

The *median* is the value at the midpoint of the list. If there are seven items, it's the value of the fourth from the top (or bottom). If there are eight items, it's the value that is halfway between the fourth item from the top and the fourth item from the bottom. It can be useful if there are some extremely high or extremely low values in the list, which would cause the mean to be far from the midpoint.

The *mode* is the value that occurs most often in the list. This assumes a large enough number of items in the list to make such a calculation meaningful. The mode is therefore often not the best representation of the average, but it can identify the most popular value.

To illustrate the difference and the mischief inherent in the difference, let's ask, What's the average sales commission earned by our salespeople? Here's the list:

Name	Commission	Rank
Adams	$4,800	(2)
Baker	3,300	(5)
Carlson	2,300	(9)
Dugan	1,600	(10)
Edwards	2,800	(7) tie
Franklin	3,600	(4)
Glover	6,900	(1)
Harris	2,800	(7) tie
Ingalls	3,000	(6)
Keller	3,800	(3)
Total	$34,900	

Luckily for us, there are 10 salespeople, which will make the calculations a bit easier. What's the mean? It's $34,900 divided by 10, or $3,490.

Calculation of the median involves finding the two values in the middle, because we have an even number of values. Fifth from the top numerically is Baker, with $3,300. Fifth from the bottom numerically is Ingalls, with $3,000. The difference between these two numbers is $300. Adding half of that difference to the lower number (or subtracting half of the difference from the higher number) gives us a median of $3,150.

The mode is easily identified; it's $2,800.

So, the three different "averages" are

Mean: $3,490

Median: $3,150

Mode: $2,800

Quite a difference. I went through this to demonstrate, one more time, that the calculation method used can bias a presentation. If I'm out to prove that the sales force is, by and large, not doing too well, I'll use the median (or the mode, if I can get away with it). If I'm trying to cast their performance in the best possible light, I'll use the mean. And either way, I'll be right.

The real mischief comes about when a report or presentation starts confusing one median with another mean. In other words, to keep yourself straight, make sure that the same calculation method was used for all the numbers being compared.

A look at the performance of Glover and Dugan convinces us that the average alone does not tell the whole story. There is considerable variation here. Statisticians call this *dispersion*. Unless you consider the dispersion in a range of numbers, the average can be misleading.

For example, a company in which the average (mean) salary is $41,600 doesn't look unusual. But, it could be that the company has nine people making $24,000 each (for a total of $216,000) plus a CEO making $200,000; the mean would be $41,600 ($416,000/10). The mean alone is misleading in that case, but that wouldn't stop someone from being proud of it in a presentation. Politicians do it all the time, particularly when they're discussing the tax code.

Dispersion usually gets measured by statisticians using the *standard deviation*. That's a formula for calculating a kind of "average" variance from the mean. Before we get there, though, let's look at the range and the real average deviation.

The *range* is simply the difference between the highest value and the lowest value on the list. In the case of our salespeople, that's $6,900 – $1,600, or $5,300. Right away, there's a red flag (or at least a yellow one): The range is greater than the mean of $3,490. The average alone does not tell the story.

The *average deviation* is a bit harder to calculate, but thanks to computer spreadsheets, it's not time consuming. We just calculate how much each individual number deviates from the mean and add them up. Notice that we're not interested in whether each number was higher or lower than the mean; we're interested only in the difference.

Here are our salespeople again. We'll first calculate how far each one is from the mean, then total the differences.

Name	Commission	Deviation
Adams	$4,800	1,310
Baker	3,300	190
Carlson	2,300	1190
Dugan	1,600	1,890
Edwards	2,800	690
Franklin	3,600	110
Glover	6,900	3,410
Harris	2,800	690
Ingalls	3,000	490
Keller	3,800	310
Total	$34,900	10,280

Remember, plus or minus is irrelevant here. Now, we divide the total deviation by the number of items: The average deviation, or variation from the mean, is 1,028.

A more complicated calculation results in the standard deviation, which is the best known measurement of dispersion. With larger numbers and a normal distribution curve, the standard deviation is more accurate than the average deviation.

The point is, the smaller the deviation (average or standard), the tighter is the information cluster. Sounds obvious. But for the normal distribution (the famous bell-shaped curve), the standard deviation means this: About 68% of the population will be within one standard deviation plus or minus from the mean; about 95% of the population will be within two standard deviations plus or minus from the mean.

Of course, that assumes that the "normal" distribution is valid for your population, which may not be the case. The normal distribution does not apply to all statistical situations. Many people have gotten into trouble trying to warp their information to fit the normal distribution, or vice versa.

That Average Just Moved!

Remember our 12-month budget, with its variations from month to month? If we're trying to keep a record of average sales (or other items) by month to track ourselves against last year, those variations can get in the way of making an accurate comparison.

For example, tracking daily sales involves differences between days of the week and weeks of the month. Mondays may be heavier than Tuesdays and Fridays. The last week of the month may be heavier than the first week. Any number of real-world conditions contribute to these fluctuations. Yet, if you try to compare this week with last week, the effort becomes almost meaningless unless you can adjust for those factors.

Enter the moving average. To get a better handle on what an "average" week should look like, add up the sales for the previous 4 weeks and divide by 4. You now have an average week against which to compare the present one. Next week, you'll drop off the oldest week and add the sales for the new one, now known as "this week." The weeks roll on, and the 4-week average moves forward. Moving averages can be used for previous weeks or previous months (usually 12) to smooth out variations.

A Few Final Words

This book is designed to point out the value of mathematical tools for marketers. You are not likely to become an expert in higher mathematics, although these disciplines can be useful. For example, calculus helps to measure rates of change, maybe before the change gets out of hand. Probability analysis supports effective decision making. (Take care that probability analysis does not replace decision making.) Linear regression analysis can explain the relative weights of factors affecting an outcome— Was it color or price or advertising or some other reason?

The point is that you don't have to become an expert in accounting, statistics, or higher mathematics if you find and hire people with these skills. What I have tried to do is sensitize you to what is possible, improve your internal baloney detectors, and remove as much of your math phobia as possible.

Concentrate on developing an understanding of costs and accounting for costs. That area is likely to have the most impact on your success. Determine and track the ratios in Appendix A. You can even make approximations of those ratios from the statements in competitors' annual reports.

Finally, determine what factors are important to your bosses. Find out how they evaluate the organization and what factors they consider to be more important than others. In the end, mathematics is a tool that will enhance not only your survival but your growth as well.

Appendix A:
A Summary of
Nonmagic Formulae

Two concepts apply to all of these formulas. First, the concept of threshold versus the concept of ranking.

Threshold means that there is a predetermined minimum (or maximum) acceptable numeric level against which the result of applying the formula will be compared. If the threshold value is not met, then no further favorable consideration will be given to the project or organization being analyzed. *Ranking* means that a number of projects or organizations will be analyzed and, after meeting the threshold, will then be compared with each other to determine their relative value or priority.

Although this may seem to be a small distinction, its importance lies in the mental approach that is brought to the analysis. The primary reason that analysts develop thresholds is to make things easier for themselves. It's a binary decision: yes/no. Do we look at this anymore or do we throw it in the discard pile and move on? Of course, we must be careful of the illusion that the threshold has some basis in fact. It is far more likely that a threshold is based on rationalization. That is, it is a value selected by the analyst (or the analyst's boss) to narrow the field or to trigger some action that will require no further thought. "If it isn't at least a 15% return, toss it out." That action would then be more easily justified as an "automatic" based on the threshold's defined "standard."

Do not assume that a given threshold value is scientifically more correct than any other; its primary virtue is that it has been accepted as meaningful. Issues involving thresholds, then, are as follows: Has the cutoff point been set too high or too low? Where is it? (If you know there's no way you'll meet it, why go through the exercise?) Can the cutoff point be changed? Can you make the argument that factors other than the ratio or formula in question should be considered even at this early stage?

Ranking based on ratios or formulas is the method used to prioritize allocation of resources. If investment decisions are based on expected profit dollars or percentage return on investment, well and good. But are the investment elements accurately valued? Has the risk or probability of reward been taken into account? What is the probability that the investment has been understated or projected returns overstated? The ratios cannot easily take that into account, although one approach is to multiply the numbers by the probability of something actually happening. Here again, we venture into subjective waters.

The formulas presented here, then, are well-known mechanical aids to assist in analysis, particularly comparison with approved standards, other projects or organizations, or other time periods. They do not replace judgment and experience, because they are based on subjective ideas about what is good or bad. As I have noted, the idea that subjective considerations guide a process usually comes as bad news, particularly to engineers. The formulas are nothing more than tools, and as with all tools, the quality of the end product depends on the skill with which they are used.

Many comparisons can be made by measuring various items of revenue and cost against sales. These percentages are often found in a separate column on an Income Statement. The percentages can then be judged against prior time periods, industry norms, or personal prejudices. The formulas are divided into operations formulas, financial ratios, and marketing ratios.

Operations Formulas

1. **Cost of Goods Sold**

**Beginning inventory + Cost of purchases +
Cost of adding value − Ending inventory**

What we sold equals what we had in inventory at the beginning of a period, plus what we bought to resell during the period, plus the costs we incurred to add value, minus what we had left in inventory at the end of the period.

The average inventory can be calculated easily or in great detail, depending on how much information you have. If all you have is an inventory at the beginning of the year and another at the end of the year, adding them up and dividing by 2 yields an average inventory. If you have monthly inventory figures, you can add them up and divide by 12 to obtain an average. True masochists will attempt to use daily figures.

Avoid the error of dividing sales by the average inventory. There is no meaningful relationship between costs and sale prices; it's a comparison of apples and oranges. While we're at it, remember that inventories are valued at "cost or market, whichever is lower."

2. Gross Margin

$$\frac{\text{Sales} - \text{Cost of Goods Sold}}{\text{Sales}}$$

Gross margin is the money we have left over after paying the direct costs of producing what we sold. With any luck, the margin is large enough to cover the other costs of operating the business and leave a profit. It is expressed as a percentage of sales. Most managers become concerned when gross margin falls below 50%, that is, when the direct costs of goods sold exceeds half of the total business costs. Comparing the gross margin for the current time period against prior periods is a useful indicator in cost control. Falling margins almost inevitably lead to "cost-containment programs," many of which are conducted without regard for customer satisfaction.

3. Inventory Turnover (Stockturn)

$$\frac{\text{Cost of Goods Sold}}{\text{Average Inventory}}$$

Stockturn is the number of times the average inventory turned over in a time period. Generally, it's a measure of how much junk you have lying around masquerading as inventory. If your cost of sales is 10 times the average inventory, you have a more efficient operation than if your cost of sales is twice your average inventory. Obviously, a smaller average inventory means lower storage costs and less capital tied up. The balance lies between velocity and efficiency, on the one hand, and not having to tell customers you're out of stock, on the other hand. Look for items that do not sell in large quantities and try judiciously to (a) reduce the amount you keep on hand or (b) see if a higher price is justified because of rarity.

It may be better to sell off or scrap some inventory and take a one-time loss rather than to keep incurring the storage and space costs. I once encountered a situation where a 50-year supply of brake shoes for a given vehicle model had been carried on the books because a manager was reluctant to show the "loss," even though the problem had started under a previous manager.

4. Marketing Contribution

Sales – Cash outlay costs

Marketing contribution is a useful calculation to determine just how much money has been or will be contributed to the organization as a result of doing a given job or putting a given product on the market. This is often called an out-of-pocket analysis. The key is that no allocated costs are included, merely the additional out-of-pocket cash payments necessary to get the job done. The premise is that the business is operating anyway and allocated or fixed costs have been or will be incurred whether the project is undertaken or not.

When comparing results or projections, the marketing contribution calculation strips away much of the confusion introduced by including allocated costs. The classic example is the railroad. If the revenues from a train exceed the out-of-pocket costs of running an additional freight train, there is a positive marketing contribution. But, in many cases, adding to the costs of this train a portion of the fixed costs of track, and so on, which do not change appreciably because of this particular train, creates a picture of unprofitability that is not real.

5. Sales per Square Foot

$$\frac{\text{Sales}}{\text{Square feet of floor space}}$$

This is a common formula used, particularly in retailing, to measure the ROI of a particular resource. Store chains can compare stores against each other or against other time periods.

I have used floor space here, but other resources can also be used for comparisons. What are the sales per employee-hour? What are the sales per expense account lunch? What are the sales per inquiry? What are the sales per advertising dollar? The list is limited only by the dimensions you may consider to be relevant.

6. Operating Profit Margin

$$\frac{\text{Profit before interest and taxes}}{\text{Sales}}$$

Operating profit margin is a percentage figure measuring profit from operations, without consideration of capital costs or taxes, both of which are beyond the control of the operating unit manager. It is the best financial measurement of a given operation's management and policies.

7. Net Profit Margin

$$\frac{\text{Profit after taxes}}{\text{Sales}}$$

Net profit margin is after-tax profits, or losses. It's the "real" dollar figure, but it measures top management rather than operating managers.

Profitability Formulas

Up to now, we have been dealing directly with sales and costs. The following formulas concern the investment of resources made to achieve the operating results. The simple question is, Would you rather earn 5% on your money or 10%?

1. Return on Assets

$$\frac{\text{(Profit after taxes)} + \text{(Interest Costs)}}{\text{Total assets invested}}$$

This is the basic measurement of ROI. If two managers show a $10,000 profit but the resources in Project A are $100,000 and Project B has $200,000 invested in it, Project A has the better rate of return.

Interest costs are often added to after-tax profits because the cost of borrowed capital for the investment is relevant to the comparison. In our example above, if Manager A had another $100,000 of borrowed capital over and above the $100,000 investment, and the interest cost on that loan was $10,000, the actual profit is only $10,000; the two come out even. If you were Manager B, wouldn't you want the calculation to reflect that?

2. Return on Equity

$$\frac{\text{Profit after taxes}}{\text{Total Stockholders' Equity}}$$

The equity component of the balance sheet, rather than the total asset, is used for this ratio. This measurement is of great interest to stockholders or owners, even though it may not accurately reflect managerial operating performance.

3. Return on Common Stock

$$\frac{\text{Profit after taxes}}{\text{Total Common Stock Equity}}$$

This is a useful ratio where there is preferred stock outstanding. Preferred stock is usually nonvoting and has a fixed dividend. That dividend is usually considered to be more like an interest payment than an equity return.

4. Earnings per Share

$$\frac{\textbf{Profit after taxes}}{\textbf{Number of shares outstanding}}$$

This is perhaps the most-used gauge of corporate profitability for holders of Common stock. Total profit is divided by the number of Common stock shares in stockholders' hands. This figure has a great impact on the actual present value of a share of stock.

5. Total Asset Turnover

$$\frac{\textbf{Sales}}{\textbf{Total Assets}}$$

Total asset turnover is a measure of the effectiveness with which a company's assets are being used to generate revenue. The average ratio for companies within an industry is most often used for comparison. Although revenue or sales does not necessarily relate to profit, asset turnover ratios can help an analyst determine whether a company's business volume is solid, growing in a healthy way, or eroding over time.

6. Fixed Assets Turnover

$$\frac{\textbf{Sales}}{\textbf{Fixed Assets}}$$

Limiting the assets used in the ratio to fixed assets highlights the efficient use of plant and equipment, independent of cash, inventory, and receivables.

Financial Ratios

1. Current Ratio

$$\frac{\textbf{Current Assets}}{\textbf{Current Liabilities}}$$

This is the basic and most often used calculation of solvency. Does the organization have enough cash and assets easily convertible to cash to pay its bills? Financial people are likely to look askance at a current ratio less than 2, that is, if current assets are not at least twice the current liabilities, there is likely to be a problem.

2. Quick Ratio (Acid Test)

$$\frac{\text{Current Assets} - \text{Inventory}}{\text{Current Liabilities}}$$

For even more conservative analysts, the assumption is that the inventory is worthless. Now, can the company still pay its bills? That's the acid test.

3. Cash Ratio

$$\frac{\text{Cash} + \text{Marketable securities}}{\text{Current Lliabilities}}$$

Now, let's remove every current asset from the calculation except cash and near-cash. That will tell us how long the company can go without further inflow of funds. That may sound extreme, but it can be useful. It can also identify cash-rich companies that may be underutilizing assets and may be tempting targets for a takeover.

4. Inventory-to-Capital Ratio

$$\frac{\text{Inventory}}{\text{Current Assets} - \text{Current Liabilities}}$$

Current assets minus current liabilities equals the amount of working capital on hand. This ratio determines how much of the working capital is tied up in inventory and therefore not available to fund operations until and unless that inventory is sold.

5. Accounts Receivable Turnover

$$\frac{\text{Annual credit sales}}{\text{Accounts Receivable}}$$

This is an interesting calculation, showing what portion of total sales is unpaid at any one time. It's a mirror image of inventory turnover, because there are costs involved in carrying receivables. Some firms look at this calculation monthly, because it can be a forecaster of possible difficulties ahead.

6. Average Collection Period

$$\frac{\text{Accounts Receivable}}{\text{Total Sales/365}}$$

How long does it take a company to collect its receivables, on the average? Or to put it another way, how many days' worth of sales are unpaid for at any time? If normal payment terms are 30 days, a result much higher than 30 could indicate credit or collection problems. Here again, a change for the worse could forecast troubles, because customers in trouble will usually begin taking longer to pay.

7. Debt to Assets Ratio

$$\frac{\text{Total debt}}{\text{Total Assets}}$$

This measures the percentage of borrowed funds used to finance the firm. The "normal" percentage varies from industry to industry, but usually any debt level above 30% will raise eyebrows.

8. Debt to Equity Ratio

$$\frac{\text{Total debt}}{\text{Total Stockholders' Equity}}$$

This is another way to measure what is owed versus what is owned.

9. Long-Term Debt-to-Equity Ratio

$$\frac{\text{Total long-term debt}}{\text{Total Stockholders' Equity}}$$

Debt comes in two forms: short term and long term. This ratio considers only the structured debt that is payable over a long period of time, not current payables such as supplies. Again, the norms vary from industry to industry, but a long-term debt over 20% will usually raise eyebrows.

10. Interest Coverage Ratio

$$\frac{\text{Profits before interest and taxes}}{\text{Total interest charges}}$$

Is the company making enough money to cover interest charges? More important, at what point would a decline in profits make the company unable to make the payments?

A more rigorous formula adds lease payments to the interest charges to include all fixed charges in the calculation.

Marketing Ratios

1. Marketing Expenses/Sales

$$\frac{\text{Marketing Expenses}}{\text{Sales}}$$

This is a simple measure of marketing expense efficiency: How much bang are we getting for our marketing bucks? This calculation is constantly being made by top management; it is a primary factor in judging the marketing effort and the marketing director. An increase over a previous period will almost certainly require (possibly extensive) explanation as to why things are getting out of hand. It pays the marketing director to keep track of this ratio and to know why it is changing and why it is not getting smaller.

Here again, the problem of allocated costs arises. Marketing expenses may include items not within the marketing director's control, such as a share of the rising cost of the CEO's yacht (which was used to entertain clients in June 1997).

2. Sales Expenses/Sales

$$\frac{\text{Sales Expenses}}{\text{Sales}}$$

This is the same simple measurement applied to the sales force. As with marketing expenses, the ratio may vary for many good reasons that are not as obvious as the ratio itself.

3. Advertising Cost per Thousand (CPM) Impressions

$$\frac{\text{Cost of advertisement}}{\text{Readers}/1,000}$$

If Magazine A charges $1,200 for a full-page ad and has 240,000 readers in whom you are interested, then $1,200/240 = $5 per thousand readers. If Magazine B charges $1,500 and has 320,000 readers of interest to you, the cost per thousand is $4.69. Despite its higher cost, Magazine B may be the better investment. Note that the calculation is based on "readers of interest to you," which is quite likely to be less than the total circulation.

The same formula can also be applied to trade show booths and can even be modified as follows:

$$\frac{\text{Cost of attending trade show}}{\text{Relevant attendees} \times \text{Probability of sales resulting}}$$

In other words, people are not necessarily customers. The probability figure is not exact. The best ones are derived from your own experience, which is why we ask customers, "How did you hear about us?"

These and many other ratios are used by analysts and consultants to gauge performance. The two basic comparisons are (1) the same organization in different time periods and (2) our organization versus other organizations. In both cases, deviations from "normal" conditions are the target of further investigation. If, for example, transportation or warranty costs are significantly higher this year than last, someone will be asking questions. It will help if you know the reason.

Of course, if transportation or warranty costs are significantly lower, that is, more favorable this year, quite often the reasons are not asked. The attitude is to "Let sleeping dogs lie." That could be a mistake. Sleeping dogs often have a nasty habit of waking up and biting you. You should be alert for unexplained changes in either direction. Lower transportation costs, for example, could be due to someone trying to cut corners by using low-bid carriers. That will lower the cost, but it is also likely to lead to longer delivery times, unreliable or late deliveries, and angry customers.

Sometimes, the comparison ratios do not include dollar figures, for example, unit sales per employee (or per employee-hour) or vehicle-miles per maintenance employee. All the comparisons are between units of input and units of output, or results.

The formulas are not magic, because there is not one correct answer. What's important is that you should think in terms of understanding the reasons for whatever variations exist, whether those variations are favorable or unfavorable.

Appendix B: Sample Chart of Accounts

Account Number	Account Name

ASSETS

Current Assets

1011	Cash on Hand
1012	Checking: Security Bank (012864-32)
1013	Checking: Central Bank & Trust (DF-865-9012)
1020	Accounts Receivable
1030	Prepaid Expenses
1100	Tax Credits
1200	Inventory

Fixed Assets

1500	Land
1600	Plant Buildings
1700	Machinery and Equipment
1900	Capitalized Expenses
1901	Incorporation Expense

LIABILITIES

Current Liabilities

2010	Accounts Payable
2020	Notes Payable: Bank
2030	Sales Taxes Payable
2040	Income Tax Payable

Account Number	Account Name
2100	Wages Payable
2120	Reserve for Vacation Pay

Fixed Liabilities

2600	Mortgage on Plant

EQUITY

3100	Common Stock
3120	Preferred Stock
3500	Retained Earnings

REVENUE

4100	Sales: Department A
4101	Returns and Allowances: Department A
4110	Sales: Department B
4111	Returns and Allowances: Department B
4120	Sales: Department C
4121	Returns and Allowances: Department C
4130	Sales: Department D
4131	Returns and Allowances: Department D
4200	Interest/Investment Income
4900	Miscellaneous Income

EXPENSES

Cost of Sales

5100	Cost of Sales: Department A
5101	Labor Costs: Product A1
5102	Materials Costs: Product A1
5110	Cost of Sales: Department B
5120	Cost of Sales: Department C
5130	Cost of Sales: Department D

General Expenses

5210	Bad Debts
5310	Accounting Expenses
5320	Bank Charges and Interest

Account Number	Account Name
5330	Insurance
5341	Property Taxes
5342	Sales Taxes
5343	Income Taxes
5345	Licenses
5350	Depreciation
5360	Shipping and Freight
5400	Utilities
5401	Electricity
5402	Gas/Steam
5403	Water
5404	Telephone
5405	Internet, Cable
5410	Rent
5450	Shop Supplies and Expenses
5451	Oils and Lubricants [See below: same number]
5453	Shop Uniforms and Linens
5455	Janitorial Expenses
5457	Indirect Shop Wages
5460	Office Expenses
5461	Office Wages
5462	Postage and Couriers
5470	Vehicle Expenses
5480	Travel
5500	Professional Services
5510	Legal Expenses
5530	Consultants
5610	Discounts
5620	Sales Commissions
5630	Advertising Expenses
5635	Advertising Agency
5640	Printing and Postage: Marketing
5710	Entertainment
5720	Donations
5990	Miscellaneous Expenses

About the Author

Peter C. Weiglin is an author, a historian, and a professional speaker on many topics. His company, Omnibus Communications, specializes in marketing strategy and communications consulting for companies in the publishing and computer fields. His clients have included Lockheed, Hundman Publishing, Hewlett-Packard, Apple Computer, and North American Van Lines. He teaches management and marketing, most recently at the University of California at Berkeley Extension, and has also worked as an auditor for a New York City-based accounting firm.

He has written, produced, and narrated several TV and radio documentaries and has written five books. During the 1970s and early 1980s, he was one of a handful of people who revolutionized the public transit industry. He was the first director of marketing for a public transit system in America and went on to become a general manager and a nationally known management adviser to troubled transit systems. He has an MBA degree from the University of Pittsburgh.

As a leisure activity, he directs the Golden Gate Radio Orchestra. He has been active in many community affairs, including a term as president of the San Mateo County (California) Arts Council.